Life After Grad School

Life After Grad School

JERALD M. JELLISON

OXFORD
UNIVERSITY PRESS

2010

OXFORD
UNIVERSITY PRESS

Oxford University Press, Inc., publishes works that further Oxford University's objective of excellence in research, scholarship, and education.

Oxford   New York
Auckland   Cape Town   Dar es Salaam   Hong Kong   Karachi   Kuala Lumpur   Madrid   Melbourne
Mexico City   Nairobi   New Delhi   Shanghai   Taipei   Toronto

With offices in
Argentina   Austria   Brazil   Chile   Czech Republic   France   Greece   Guatemala   Hungary   Italy
Japan   Poland   Portugal   Singapore   South Korea   Switzerland   Thailand   Turkey   Ukraine
Vietnam

Copyright © 2010 by Oxford University Press, Inc.

Published by Oxford University Press, Inc.
198 Madison Avenue, New York, New York 10016

www.oup.com

Oxford University Press is a registered trademark of Oxford University Press, Inc.

Library of Congress Cataloging-in-Publication Data

Jellison, Jerald M., 1942–
  Life after grad school/by Jerald M. Jellison.
     p. cm.
  ISBN-13: 978-0-19-973430-6
  ISBN-10: 0-19-973430-5
  1. Business—Vocational guidance. 2. Job hunting. 3. Career development. I. Title.
  HF5381.J479 2010
  650.14—dc22
                                                              2009043482

---

1 2 3 4 5 6 7 8 9
Printed in the United States of America on acid-free paper

Note to Readers
This publication is designed to provide accurate and authoritative information in regard to the subject matter covered. It is based upon sources believed to be accurate and reliable and is intended to be current as of the time it was written. It is sold with the understanding that the publisher is not engaged in rendering legal, accounting, or other professional services. If legal advice or other expert assistance is required, the services of a competent professional person should be sought. Also, to confirm that the information has not been affected or changed by recent developments, traditional legal research techniques should be used, including checking primary sources where appropriate.

(Based on the Declaration of Principles jointly adopted by a Committee of the American Bar Association and a Committee of Publishers and Associations.)

To my wife Lucinda

Acknowledgements

Many people contributed to making this book a reality. Robert Arkin, and his network, made it possible to find a supportive publisher. Lori Handelman, the editor, has been an extraordinary champion of this book. She too made the trip from A to B. Peggy Clark provided the initial impetus for the framework of the book. I'm deeply grateful for the help and friendship of these people.

Henry Head went out of his way to put me in touch with scores of graduate students who are now successful in business. Richard Eisinger made me aware of the great career opportunities in government. Eileen Kohan's commitment to helping students forge a career path has been an instructive model. The realistic perspective and encouragement of Margaret Gatz kept me focused. Julena Lind provided insights into the role of graduate school administrators.

I am indebted to a number of people who helped me understand the point of view of contemporary graduate students and the hiring process. These include: Gary Perez, Graeme S. Fraser, the people of Dow Agro Sciences, Paromita Kar, Deborah Smith, Jeffrey Brown, Jacob and Naomi Glen-Levin, Dorian Singh, Mat Savelli, Emily Cohen, and Dennis Smith.

The constant support and invaluable editorial assistance of Lucinda Irwin Smith brought vitality to this book. *Life After Grad School* owes its life to her.

Preface

Are you thinking of changing from academics to business? Making the transition is a major life choice. You'll be moving from a known to an unknown culture.

I made the switch, and have several decades of experience in each domain. My years as a researcher, teacher, and advisor were deeply gratifying. As a professor, I knew very little about business. When I began the transition, I was suspicious and somewhat critical of business. I was blind to the many opportunities and rewards available. Now I look back in amazement. My life has been greatly enhanced because I made the change.

Up until now, you've probably been focused on getting a tenure-track job. As a result, you may be unaware that you *already* possess the knowledge and skills that could make you a very attractive candidate for a job with a corporation, government agency, or nonprofit organization. However, the process of searching for a job in business is very different from academics. To be successful, you'll need to understand this process and optimize the way you present your qualifications.

Life After Grad School is a very practical book. Brief and easy to read, each chapter is loaded with useful tools and tips. It explains what you'll need to do and then shows you exactly how to do it. The book's chapters are arranged in chronological order. It begins with making the decision to go into business, and results in receiving a job offer.

The initial chapters will help frame your decision to pursue a career in business, and the remaining chapters will guide you through the steps necessary to become a competitive and successful job candidate. You'll learn to repackage (i.e., brand) yourself in the language of business. You'll learn to highlight certain aspects of your graduate school education, and to downplay others.

The **how to** portion of the book outlines in explicit detail how to:

- write a great resume
- craft a winning elevator pitch
- define your career goals
- create a network of business contacts
- locate free job search resources
- search and apply for jobs
- handle difficult interview questions

By following the simple guidelines, you'll not only change your career but also your life's path. You'll discover more about yourself and the opportunities that are within your grasp. While a job is the proximal goal, the distal target is feeling satisfied in your career, and with yourself.

Instead of finding the business world pedestrian and uninteresting, I discovered the complex challenges of creating solutions to real-world problems. Turning ideas into results required all my creative intelligence. I found business to be as stimulating and rewarding as academia. Are you ready to get on with your life? I'm ready to help you create a better future.

Contents

SECTION III: CREATING A TRANSITION TOOLKIT

SECTION IV: LANDING YOUR JOB

Introduction

You pick up a copy of *Life After Grad School* and ask: How can this book help me? This question is also of prime concern to business people when they consider moving in a new strategic direction. They call it ROI (return on investment). If I follow this new path, what will I get in return for my investment of time, money, and resources?

Your ROI on *Life After Grad School* will be practical advice on how to get a job outside academia. The book is tailored to the needs of graduate students, and is written by someone who understands the psychology of making major changes. It's written in a way that respects your intelligence and your sincere desire to learn about business. You'll also get an honest and supportive appraisal of the opportunities and challenges of switching to business.

There are several ways to approach this book. You can read the chapters consecutively, or you can pick and choose. If you are just beginning to think about the decision to change careers, you'll definitely want to start with the first section of chapters. If you've already committed to a career in business, or have considerable experience in business, you may want to focus more on the tools and techniques detailed in the next three sections. The book is designed for grad students in all academic disciplines, with or without graduate degrees. As a result, an example that has meaning to some readers may not have relevance to others.

The phrase *Getting From Academics to Business* is shorthand for the transition you're about to make. As with any generalization, it blurs some important distinctions. The A stands for a tenure-track professor's job. Within A are the grey areas that include short-term contract teaching at the college level, and university research positions funded by soft-money grants.

The B refers to jobs in a wide range of non-academic settings. Business refers to jobs with for-profit companies, nonprofit organizations, federal, state, and local governments, and nongovernmental organizations (NGOs). The word *business* can refer to an economic activity, or to a particular organization. In this second usage, the word *business* is used interchangeably with the words *company, corporation, organization*, and *firm*.

Life After Grad School will give you an honest appraisal of what it will be like to change from an academic to a business career. You won't get an inflated picture of either the ease with which you'll get a job, or the six-digit salary you'll earn your first year. Instead, you'll get the straight story from someone who made the transition. Until now, you have been working toward a career in academics. Switching to business doesn't mean starting over from zero, but there will be some hurdles. In the long run, your graduate training will enable you to more than make up for these initial challenges.

When people are seeking employment, they're sometimes so desperate that they'll follow any lead. There are many unscrupulous individuals ready to take advantage of your situation. They'll offer to do all the work for you—write your resume, give you access to great job listings, etc. Be very cautious of websites and counselors promising miracles. Too often you get little or nothing for your money. You can find a job yourself, and *Life After Grad School* will show you how. You'll find an annotated bibliography of books on careers and the job search process on the website, JobsA2B.com.

JobsA2B.com contains a wealth of information that will help with your job search. Here are some of the things you'll find:

- Annotated bibliography of business and career books
- List of websites relevant to business and careers
- Warnings of fraudulent ads
- Examples of other grad students' resumes
- Examples of cover letters and thank you notes
- Dictionary of common business words, phrases, and concepts
- Discussion forums for grad students seeking jobs
- Connections with grad students who successfully changed from A to B
- Resume wall that's searched by firms hiring grad students
- Job wall featuring positions suited to grad students.

This website is meant to help all grad students. If you have ideas, tips, or stories you'd like to share, please forward them to **jellison@usc.edu.**

A major career change presents many challenges. The millions of people who have completed the journey from A to B want to encourage and assist you. We know you can do it.

Leaving the Academic World

I

Can You Go From A to B?

Your major professor asks you to participate in the evaluation of two under-graduates who are applying for fall admission to your program. You're flattered to be consulted on such an important decision, and you're eager to read each candidate's application.

The first applicant has off-the-chart GRE scores. Although she attended an Ivy League school and graduated *summa cum laude,* she majored in chemistry and you're in a neuroscience program. She took only a few neuroscience courses and has no research experience. The other candidate has very high, but not superlative, test scores, as well as a good GPA from a large Midwestern university. He not only majored in your field, he also has a great deal of experience conducting neuroscience research with professors and grad students.

While both applicants are very bright, Candidate A is clearly more intel-lectually gifted. Candidate B knows the field and understands exactly what he's getting into. He's already so laboratory savvy, he could immediately begin helping with research. Before recommending either or both candidates, examine the process you would use to choose the better candidate.

Now, apply your experience evaluating grad school candidates to the world of business. A company is hiring a new employee and they're conducting second interviews with the two candidates who have made it to the final selection. The two have many similarities. Both are intelligent, hardworking, responsible, and have good interpersonal skills. There are, however, a few small but significant differences.

- Candidate A has truly superior analytic skills. She can quickly assimilate new information, and she's very creative and mature.

- Candidate B has a history of working in the industry. His job skills are directly relevant to the position. He could step right in and begin producing. (Candidate A has virtually no work history).

Which candidate will be selected, and why? Will the company hire the very intelligent, quick study, or the less sophisticated but more technically qualified candidate?

Sometimes an organization needs an individual with particular skills and experience. In such business situations, Candidate B is the obvious choice. His knowledge of the industry and his precise fit with the company's needs are invaluable.

Just as frequently, an individual's long-term contribution is more important than their short-term productivity, so Candidate A is the better choice. This is especially true when an organization is hiring someone they hope to groom as a future manager or leader. In these cases, employers seek bright, creative people who are flexible and enjoy learning. These qualities are often more important than specific business experience. The company can give you training and experience, but they can't instill talents you don't already possess. Companies hire *potential*. This means they're often willing to invest time and money in training someone whose value will increase. Many CEOs use a hiring policy that is similar to the one voiced by Bill Gates: "I hire the smartest people."

Companies need the qualifications of both Candidate A and Candidate B. When you consider all the possible organizations who are hiring at any one time, both types of candidates will find their niche and succeed. From a macro perspective, getting a job is not a zero sum game.

Consider this: You are Candidate A. You already have the attributes sought by many employers. The same abilities and personal qualities that earned you admission to graduate school will also make it possible for you to get a good job in the business world. Additionally, you undoubtedly have many distinctive characteristics (i.e., personality traits, skills, interests, and life experiences) that will prove advantageous as you interview for specific jobs. For example, if you were raised in Texas, your knowledge of that region might be very valuable to one firm, while another company might hire you because you speak Spanish. Even the many hours you spend playing computer games could work in your favor if you interview with a company in the video game industry.

There are many reasons to justify the assertion that any competent grad student should be able to get a good job in business. Whether or not they get a job, and how long it takes, depends largely on how they go about the job search process. Getting a good job requires knowledge of the hiring process and a detailed plan for how to be the person selected.

When businesses try to answer strategic questions, they often utilize a SWOT analysis. There are many acronyms in the business world, and this is one you'll hear repeatedly. SWOT (pronounced like the thing we do to pesky flies) stands for *Strengths, Weaknesses, Opportunities,* and *Threats.* Just as businesses regularly conduct a SWOT analysis to help determine their future, you can use the same tool to decide how to move forward.

Strengths

Graduate students across a wide range of academic disciplines share many remarkable traits. As you read the following list, think about yourself. How do you rate in comparison to *all* people in your own age group (not just all grad students, but all of your same-age cohorts)?

Critical thinking – You grasp abstract concepts using different points of view.

Learn quickly – You digest large amounts of information and identify underlying themes, ideas, assumptions, and patterns.

Technological savvy – You use information technology at work and home.

Quantitative skills – You understand mathematics and statistical tools.

Research skills – You can design, conduct, and analyze empirical research.

Writing – You clearly and concisely express ideas in understandable language.

Oral communication – You speak with confidence and clarity.

Language fluency – You read, speak, or write in more than one language.

Ethical – You live up to your moral and ethical beliefs.

Idea exchange – You logically propose ideas and handle challenging questions.

Innovative – You look at things from novel perspectives and create new ideas.

Flexible – You're willing to explore new ideas and adopt new work practices.

Maturity – You put business first, and put the group's interests above your own.

Responsible – You meet deadlines and live up to commitments.

Hardworking – You do what is necessary to achieve goals, despite surprises.

Interpersonal skills – You put people at ease and are comfortable working with individuals from diverse backgrounds.

Teamwork – You are both a good leader and follower. You can resolve conflicts.

Political savvy – You work with and around big egos. You can build alliances.

How do you rate yourself relative to the competition? You are well above average on almost every one of these important dimensions. You have the attributes companies want, and you'll use these same strengths to make the transition into business.

Weaknesses

You, the typical graduate student, possess many talents that will enable you to distinguish yourself in business throughout your career. While these traits will be important in the long run, they won't necessarily set you apart during the initial hiring and selection process. The job market is highly competitive, especially for the really top jobs. Dozens of applicants will be as smart, hard working, and tech savvy as you. Unless your expertise matches the company's exact needs, you'll have to find ways to outshine your competitors. You can begin by examining your weaknesses.

You have two major weaknesses, but your most glaring deficiency is your lack of work experience in the business world. Unless you worked to pay your way through undergraduate school, you may not have been employed full time. You may try to convince an interviewer that your limited work experience is actually an advantage. You haven't acquired any negative habits, and you're more malleable to a company's way of doing business. This argument is not completely convincing, but you'll earn points for your panache. Grad students with substantial work experience can rely on their record of employment to substantiate their qualifications.

There are several ways to compensate for your lack of business experience. Work you have done as a teaching or research assistant may be relevant to particular jobs. Later chapters describe techniques for recasting these grad school experiences into the language of business. You'll also learn ways to build a work history and enhance your business credentials *while* you are still in grad school.

Although you have many stellar attributes, your *second* weakness is your lack of understanding about how to actually get a job in business. The procedure for hiring a new professor is very different from the employment process in business. The chapters in Sections III and IV provide detailed advice on how to succeed at the crucial steps of the business hiring process.

Opportunites

The good news is that there are opportunities to use your research, teaching, and communications talents outside academics. The business world hires individuals with abilities that are similar to the skills you acquired in graduate school. Consulting firms (a growth area in the U. S. economy) actually sell their employees' knowledge to other businesses. If your content expertise fits their market niche, there is a good chance you could be hired by a consulting firm. Even if your academic discipline isn't the same as the consulting firm's specialty, they often hire bright, hard working people and then teach them how to apply the firm's proprietary knowledge, systems, and data.

Research

Both large and small companies conduct research. If you're hired by such a firm, you might be able to use the same methodologies you employed in your academic research. The exact nature and goal of the research will be slightly different, because businesses develop products that can be profitably sold in the marketplace. Professors in disciplines where their research has ready business applications (e.g., biotech, engineering, information systems) often transfer back and forth between jobs in business and academics.

There are also companies whose sole business is doing research for other companies. In the biological arena, these firms provide cost effective services for companies that don't maintain their own laboratories. Similarly, many small firms provide market research services to other companies. Market research draws heavily on the methodologies commonly used in the social sciences.

Government departments have elaborate research facilities. This research often requires a knowledge of the physical, biological, and social sciences. The expertise of geologists and chemists is relevant to environmental issues. Life scientists and health experts are needed to explicate disease mechanisms, and social scientists are used to study worker safety and health practices. Government agencies are always hiring people to help conduct research on topics related to the environment, agriculture, defense, and health care. People are also needed to monitor the effectiveness of government-sponsored projects, and to conduct program evaluation research.

Education

If you prefer teaching to research, then the field of education can potentially yield many career paths. One clear possibility is to teach in public and private schools, prep schools, or community colleges. The people who teach in these settings are responsible for some of the most important work in the country. Although these jobs are often underappreciated, teachers can take justifiable pride and satisfaction in their career choice.

While you're considering educational opportunities, don't overlook the business world. Business organizations spend more money each year on education than the tuition dollars of all U. S. colleges and universities combined. You might skim right past these jobs because in the business world, education is commonly referred to as "training" or "development."

In the 1990s, many companies discovered they were providing so much education, they opted to centralize it under one entity. The inflated word they selected for these units was "university" (e.g., University of Toyota). Lacking research, athletic teams, or a marching band, these corporate universities consolidated educational programs ranging from technical training to advanced management courses.

Corporate universities have become increasingly popular. As of 2001, there were over 2,500 corporate universities. As the number continues to grow, more and more teachers will be needed. These instructors, trainers, or facilitators (as they are called in business) obviously don't teach the same subjects found in a normal undergraduate curriculum. The courses could involve technical information, or they could focus on the development of management, interpersonal, or communication skills.

For technical courses, individuals who already possess this type of expertise and experience are taught the most effective methods for instructing other employees. For example, when Toyota introduced the new Prius hybrid, several dozen exceptional mechanics were trained in the new technology. These experts taught the repair technicians in all of Toyota's 1,400 local dealerships.

While you won't be hired to teach hybrid automotive repair, you could be hired to teach courses that relate to managing people. Companies will hire you because of your proven effectiveness in the classroom, and because you can quickly learn the course's content.

Can you picture yourself in a "train the trainer" program? These programs are crafted in great detail by instructional design professionals. The typical undergraduate course looks anemic by comparison. You'll learn the necessary content, and you'll then use your classroom skills to effectively teach the company's employees.

It's not just a company's *own* employees that need education; firms often provide education for the customers who purchase and use their products and services. Businesses that sell complex machinery and software platforms provide educational services to insure the products will be used properly and safely.

By now you've probably guessed that almost every activity occurring in business also takes place in government. Government agencies provide far-reaching educational programs for their employees, as well as for private citizens. If you love teaching, you'll want to search for teaching jobs in government as well as in business.

Communication and Management

If your talents lie in the realm of communication, you'll find innumerable opportunities in both business and government. Every major organization has a department of communication. All organizations regularly use a variety of media to communicate with their customers, employees, stockholders, and with the general public. Since it is vitally important for government and corporate entities to get their messages out effectively, people with excellent communication skills are always needed.

In addition to your research, teaching, and communication skills, do you also have a talent for organizing and motivating people? Have you ever thought you might some day want to become the chair of an academic department, or even a dean? If so, this suggests you may be able to translate this capacity for leadership into business.

Business and academia employ different lexicons when describing jobs that involve managerial skills. While the words may differ, the terms refer to similar activities. Someone who oversees an academic department is called a chair, while department heads in business are called managers. Deans are in charge of a group of departments, as well as their chairs. In business, individuals with comparable responsibilities would be called general managers or vice presidents. Instead of a university president, corporations have a CEO (i.e., Chief Executive Officer). Just slightly lower on the hierarchy of authority are individuals at what is called the C-level (e.g., Chief Financial Officer; Chief Operations Officer; Chief Information Officer; Chief Learning Officer, etc.)

Every organization needs people to orchestrate and supervise the activities of managers. A company might hire you for your potential leadership talents and abilities, rather than for your specific knowledge or experience. As a management trainee, you might enter a training program that includes a six-to twelve-month assignment in various company departments at different locations. During this period you'll learn the ins and outs of the organization, as well as the operational structure of the company. At the same time, your performance is being evaluated. After your training is completed, you'll be placed in a fulltime management position.

Alternatively, you might also be hired for a specific skill set (i.e., research, teaching, and communication) and over time, your supervisors would recognize your management capabilities. When a vacancy opens in your department, you might be promoted to manager. In this new capacity, you'd be directing and overseeing your former work group. As you continue to demonstrate your effectiveness, more opportunities and promotions will move you to higher levels of management.

Threats

The central message of this chapter is that you have every reason to be optimistic about switching from the academic to the business world. There's enough evidence to prove that your abilities will qualify you for a good starting job. There are a wide range of job opportunities available in business, government, and nonprofit organizations. So far, it's sounding pretty good. What possible threats could possibly block your success?

For a moment, let's go back to the beginning of this chapter. You were asked to evaluate two undergraduate applicants for a coveted place in graduate school. Imagine that you actually have the opportunity to interview each candidate. You ask the woman, "How will majoring in chemistry affect your success in neuroscience?" She claims to feel very well prepared for neuroscience on the basis of her chem training and her two intro-level neuroscience courses (she did earn an A in both). She is confident she won't encounter any problems. She is a very quick learner and is prepared to work diligently in order to compensate for any deficiencies in her knowledge.

When you ask about her lack of research experience, she asserts that the skills she developed in her chem labs will readily transfer to neuroscience research. If she encounters any problems, she'll be able to quickly learn the new lab techniques.

She estimates that by the end of the first semester, she'll be completely up to speed. As a seasoned grad student, you understand how much there is to learn about your field and how much time was required before you mastered the lab. After the interview, what is your reaction to this candidate? Are you as confident as she is that she can do the work? In a job interview, could you mistakenly express the same degree of inflated self-confidence?

Are you familiar with the expression, "Mind the Gap"? This uniquely British phrase serves as a warning in London's underground subway stations. Sometimes there is an unexpectedly wide space between the edge of the boarding platform and the subway car entrance—the gap. By being mindful and paying careful attention, able-bodied people can easily step across the gap from the platform to the subway car.

Metaphorically, there is a gap between your starting location on the academic "platform" and the entryway to the business "car." This gap can be far wider, and more challenging, than merely a single step. If your confidence turns into *overconfidence* it will threaten your chances of getting a job. Many academics convey an air of superiority that is not appreciated in business. Your attitude could be your greatest threat. Overly confident individuals are often completely unaware of their self-sabotage.

Balance your optimism and self-confidence with a measure of realistic humility. You have a lot to learn. You will face many challenges—not only getting a job, but succeeding once you're employed. Although you have many good employment prospects, people won't beg you to join their company. Nor will you waltz right into your dream job. It will take work.

By changing careers, you enter a foreign domain. This book will serve as a guide so the path won't be as taxing or as long.

2

The Path of Change

This is big—really big. Changing careers from academics to business is a major life transition. This change takes on an even greater significance if you've always wanted to be a professor. Your whole identity is in flux. You've told everyone you're going to be a professor. It felt good when you said "professor," and you could sense an increase in people's respect. The hopes you've talked about with friends, the dreams you've imagined, are all being dashed. While you don't have a clear image of your future, you're fully aware of the life you're about to give up.

You know academia and you like it. Much of your adult life has been lived in this small world. You've been successful here, and now you're giving it up. What are you going to tell people? Your feelings of loss and grief are probably mixed with feelings of self-doubt. It's frightening to realize you have no idea where you're going, and you have many questions about how to get there.

These thoughts and feelings are normal. They're typical of how everyone feels when a change involves loss. You can observe these feelings in people who are experiencing the loss of a loved one, the end of a romantic relationship, or the rejection of a research paper or book proposal. Change hurts, and big changes hurt even more.

Time cures all wounds. Maybe, but it can take a long time. You want relief *now*. While the pain and confusion can't be immediately banished, there are things you can do to help. You can minimize your negative thoughts and emotions, and therefore move through the change more quickly. A person's reactions to change follow a predictable progression. By learning to recognize the stage you're currently traversing, you'll be able accept your feelings as normal and natural. Rather than being debilitated by these feelings, you'll be able to acknowledge them. You'll gain a degree of control, rather than letting your emotions absorb all your energy. You'll learn to recognize what you are experiencing at the moment and *still* be able to take the small steps necessary to accomplish your goals. You'll begin to gain more control when you understand the human dimensions of change.

You can picture your personal path through this change from A to B by visualizing a J curve (see Figure 2.1). Think of the journey in topographic terms. You're starting on the level academic plateau to the left. You must go over the cliff and down into the valley before you make the long ascent up to the mountaintop of business on the right. The first half of the change process is much more difficult than the second half.

Our reactions to a major life change follow a predictable progression of five stages. The J-Curve of Change maps the common thoughts and feelings linked to each stage of change. Stage 1 is called Static Quo. You're currently at Stage 1—a graduate student. On the career front, there is stasis in your life because you've been a student for several years. At some point, that steady state was jarred by the idea of leaving the academic world. If you always planned to be a professor, the mere thought of a detour can be disruptive. As you begin to seriously contemplate a career shift, you may simultaneously begin to entertain these thoughts:

"I really like the academic environment. I don't want to give it up."

"Why would I make this switch?"

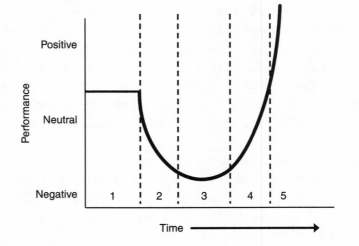

FIGURE 2.1 The J-Curve of Change

"How will I get a job in business?"

"Could I actually make the transition?"

"Even if I did, would I like it?"

These anxiety-provoking questions arouse fears that are commonly associated with the anticipation of any major change.

The first steps are the hardest. The most frightening part of the journey is starting over the steep cliff and descending into Stage 2. Think of it as an emotional cliff. It feels as though you are stepping off into a completely unknown world. But wait—is it really unknown to you? Even though you've never worked in business, you have preconceived ideas about what to expect.

When we step into the realm of the unknown, we often imagine the worst. Do you remember when you were falling asleep as a child? You envisioned all kinds of monsters and ghosts in the unknown darkness. Did you know where they were in the room (hint: closet and under the bed) and what they were going to do to you? Now that you're a grad student, your monsters go under the banner of failure:

"Who would want to hire me? I don't know anything about business."

"People will laugh at me. I'll be humiliated."

"Instead of being a creative scientist or intellectual, I'll become a cog in the vast world of business."

Your whole life starts to feel meaningless, and new horrors come to mind:

"My professors and grad school friends are going to ostracize me."

"If anyone finds out I'm even thinking about switching, I could get kicked out of the degree program."

Eventually, in spite of your fears, a sense of urgency, combined with curiosity, drives you to take the first steps over the cliff. Although the experience isn't as frightening as you imagined, you nevertheless stumble a bit as you begin the descent through Stage 2. A counselor at the career center calls your resume "thin," and you sense he's pessimistic about your job prospects. You are rebuffed when you call a few people to seek their help. When you finally find an ally who supports your decision, you're nervous and flummoxed. You ask dumb questions and ramble on when they inquire about your plans.

As you slink back to your apartment, you think:

"Who am I kidding?"

"This is a colossal mistake."

"I'll never make it in the business world."

"Maybe I don't need a job. I'll live with my parents for a few months."

These thoughts wreak havoc with your self-confidence. You experience all kinds of negative feelings, including confusion, apprehension, regret, and even panic. This is Stage 2—and, as advertised, it's hard. So hard that you convince yourself to stay in academics. You slam on the business brakes and resolve to write more research papers and apply for a small grant. You immediately begin to feel better. You know that when the grant comes through, you'll be a shoo-in for a tenure-track job.

Stage 2 is where most grad students throw in the proverbial towel. Because uncertainty, mistakes, rejection, and a lack of control are things we'd all rather avoid, we retreat. Instead of continuing to take small steps to learn more about business, you try to escape into your former dreams. You imagine the things you might do to make a professor's job materialize. You know someone out there must want you.

In the business world, this type of reaction is called "buyer's remorse." It's a common reaction after signing the contract for any big-ticket item (e.g., a new car, a house, or even a spouse). When you were driving around in your old clunker, all you thought about were the benefits of having a better car. Now that it's in your driveway, you focus on the costs—high monthly payments, increased insurance, and bigger repair bills. It's normal to start thinking your 15-year-old gas-guzzler wasn't so bad.

If, instead of giving up, you continue (in spite of your doubts) to move toward a job in business, you'll soon discover your forays are getting easier. A few things are starting to go your way. You're becoming adept at asking the kinds of questions that encourage people to give you constructive advice. Slowly at first, but then more frequently, you're beginning to use the jargon of business.

You are entering Stage 3 of the change process—the arc down at the bottom of the J. Your small successes are growing and your mistakes are decreasing.

Unfortunately, you still suffer setbacks and dead ends. Progress doesn't happen as quickly as you'd like, so it's easy to become discouraged. There's only a little solace in the fact that things aren't getting any worse. Because you haven't achieved your ultimate goal of landing a job, you may think you aren't making any progress. But, you *are* making progress. You're learning a great deal, and you're making important gains. People often attribute their small victories to luck. It's not just luck—you're learning what works and what doesn't in this new environment.

If a good day is followed by a bad day, your hopes can be dashed. These are normal feelings. Be prepared for the call of the siren trying to lure you back to academia. This temptation is natural. Of course you'd like to escape from an unpleasant situation. You can experience these urges and still accomplish one or two small things every day.

At last you receive some really great news. You're called for a job interview. Even though you know you aren't qualified, this opportunity dramatically changes your outlook. Although you don't get hired, the interviewers are very complimentary. They even give you a lead for a job they believe will better suit your talents. These positive results move you into Stage 4 of the J curve. You begin to look at yourself and the world in a new light:

"I'm getting the hang of this, and I'm doing better than I thought."

"This is going to happen. Maybe not today, but someday, I *will* get a job."

"Learning about business is actually fun. I have a knack for it."

You're becoming much more polished and assertive when you meet business people. You enjoy conquering the small challenges of this previously mysterious and forbidden world.

Then at last comes *the* day. You're called back for a second interview. You talk with several people on the team. You like them, and they appear to like you. That evening you receive the call you once thought was impossible. You are their top candidate. They want you. You are offered a job and it's a good job. Your thoughts and feeling are transformed:

"I did it. And I did it on my own."

"I can be a success."

"Bring it on, world—I'm up to the challenge."

Congratulations! You're in Stage 5 of the J Curve. Your feelings are incomparable. All of your work and tribulations were worthwhile. You're filled with confidence. You're proud of yourself and you feel a real sense of accomplishment.

From this new vantage point you have a radically different perspective on your past and your future. When you are securely at the top of the mountain, you can look back to where you started. You may have trouble understanding why you had such a negative attitude about making the change. There are many opportunities ahead and you're elated.

Most major changes follow this path of the J-Curve, whether we choose to make the change or it's forced on us. As we progress through the stages of change, we experience a vast array of thoughts and feelings. Some people try to deny and suppress these feelings, while others exaggerate the negativity and wallow in pain and self-pity. Action is the answer. You must keep moving forward. Don't worry about how much work lies ahead. Don't focus on the past. Regret will only slow your progress. You have no evidence that your picture of what might have been, would have actually happened. This book encourages you to focus on the small steps, and shows you how to keep taking constructive action.

Many people have made the journey. Find inspiration in their success and learn from their experiences. The mistakes of others will enable you to avoid many hazards along the way.

This book will equip you with the critical tools needed for your journey. You'll learn how to build a business network. Primed with a brief script, you'll be able to quickly and professionally introduce yourself when you meet a potential contact. You'll begin using the multiple routes to a job in business. When you go on a job interview, you won't be excessively nervous. You'll be able to anticipate the questions and respond with answers that demonstrate you have what it takes. Interviewers will be impressed with your thoughtfulness, honesty, and your vitality.

You may be one of the fortunate few hired after your first venture into the business marketplace. As much as you may wish for it, this is an extremely low-probability event. For most people, the path will take longer and will come with many of the feelings and experiences catalogued above.

Although Stages 2 and 3 can be fraught with obstacles, this is also where a person's finest qualities can come to the fore. Resilience, adaptability and creativity flourish when you tackle barriers, missteps and setbacks. Obstructions can be frustrating, but they'll force you to develop new ways of achieving your goals. In grad school you learned discipline, determination, and a work ethic. These traits will enable you to master the changes ahead.

3

To B or Not to B?

Just as Hamlet contemplated the great unknown in his famous soliloquy, you too are pondering your future. Fortunately, the issue you face doesn't have the life-and-death severity of Hamlet's. You have good reason to be optimistic. *To B—To enter Business—or Not? That is the question.*

Before you begin the change process discussed in Chapter 2, you have to honestly tackle this question: are you ready to explore your options in the business world, or do you still have one foot in academics? It's time to honestly assess where you stand. Is now the best time to read this book and prepare for a major life change?

People have different stances toward this question.

1.   Some have already closed the door on academics and are prepared to give 100% to their new career.
2.   Others have privately concluded that business is a better option, but haven't announced this decision publicly. They act as though their interest in business is idle curiosity.
3.   Some want to remain in academics, but decide to learn more about business as a possible back-up plan (Plan B).
4.   A few will become professors with absolutely no interest in a business career.

Even if you sincerely want a job in academics, it's always wise to keep your options open. Extraneous events can determine whether you complete your Ph.D. and get a tenure-track position. Your thoughts about a business career may have only developed during your years in grad school. See if you can place yourself and your fellow students in one of these general categories ("market segments" in the language of business).

Undecided. Some students enroll in grad school even though they're completely uncertain about the occupational path they hope to follow. They may enroll simply because they don't have any alternatives. These students often make a detour during their first or second year.

Diverted. Although a student may be truly committed to academics, extenuating circumstances in their personal life may require that they focus their time and attention on family issues, relationship problems, or health concerns. They might take a leave of absence. While they genuinely plan to return to school, many of them do not.

Discouraged. As some students move forward, they must face a harsh reality about their future. They probably aren't going to become professors. At first, they don't want to accept this conclusion, so they continue their coursework and research. Gradually, they become less and less engaged. They grow more engaged with other activities— i.e., working as a T.A., mentoring undergraduates, or off-campus involvements. Although they finish all the required courses, they never complete the dissertation.

Determined. Another group of students remain actively committed to meeting all of the requirements for their Ph.D. They complete the dissertation with the full realization that they will not be able to get a fulltime job as a professor. They want the degree, regardless. By focusing on their research, they can avoid thinking about the future. Some will continue as researchers on soft money grants, or work as contract teachers at small colleges.

Doctor/professors. These are the individuals who prevail over all the obstacles. If they gain tenure, they'll probably spend their entire career completely inside the academic world.

The advice in this book will prove worthwhile for *all* these students. The book will be of practical benefit to people who are *undecided*. Instead of drifting through another year of school, they'll begin to seriously explore other options. For the people who become *distracted* by an unexpected personal crisis, this book will provide a step-by-step guide on how to build a career outside academics. Students who are *discouraged* about their prospects in academia should delve into these chapters ASAP. They'll discover constructive alternatives to academics, and they'll gain a renewed sense of purpose. **Determined** students must be admired for their diligence (a skill that will prove vital when they decide to go from A to B). This book will help them plan a life after grad school. **Doctor/professors** should keep the book on their shelf in case they don't get tenure. Or, in few years, they may decide they'd like to explore the larger world outside the university.

Deciding between academics and business requires an objective assessment of the benefits and costs of each career path. If you've never worked in business, it's difficult to be objective. Although I've had decades of experience in both domains, my perspective represents only one point of view. Combine the information in this book with the opinions of people who know both tracks, and you'll have a more complete context for your decision.

Advantages of Being a Professor

The life of a professor at a major university can have many benefits. The opportunity to research your own theoretical ideas is a rare privilege. Publishing one's theories and findings for colleagues around the world can be deeply satisfying. Being part of a continuing multi-generational effort that expands our common knowledge provides a connection to all humanity.

Teaching both undergraduate and graduate students offers many sources of pleasure. It's wonderful to have an audience that not only listens, but writes down what you say. You experience a tremendous sense of fulfillment when you connect with a classroom of young people. It's very gratifying to work one-on-one with a student during office hours, and it's even more satisfying to watch students aspire to higher levels of performance. The rewards are said to be intangible, but they can give meaning to your life.

And, as if these benefits aren't enough to make academics worthwhile, there are many practical considerations. The three-month summer vacation is unheard-of outside teaching. The job security once you earn tenure becomes a quiet comfort. Also, many professors enjoy immersing themselves in the intellectual and cultural environment of the university. Society's high regard for professors won't pay the bills, but it's another perk.

Let's face it—"professor" is a very attractive package. No wonder we all dreamed of this life. There are many good reasons to choose an academic career. Speaking from personal experience, I can attest it's been a wonderful life.

If you have an unshakeable drive to become a professor, you must follow your passion. You'll never be content unless you fully commit to pursuing your goal of an academic job. If you're convinced this is the only life that will make you happy, then go for it.

Disadvantages of Being a Professor

To be fair and balanced, a chapter on the benefits of academics must include a discussion of the flip side—the drawbacks. To get a more accurate appraisal of the negative aspects of the academic path, interviews were conducted with grad students who had recently moved to a career in business. The goal was to identify the many factors that had influenced their career choice. Some of their reasons may not apply to you, but a few of their observations may resonate.

If you are hired as a starting assistant professor you'll need to make a total commitment to your work for five or six years. In the interviews, many former grad students cited the demands of gaining tenure as a negative. The standards for granting tenure keep getting higher. Once it was enough to get a grant; now, grants only count if the funding amount is astronomical. The work, plus the stress, and putting your life on hold, was too high a price for many former grad students.

In order to have a more accurate sense of the pressures associated with gaining tenure, talk with recent hires in your department, whether or not they're in your sub-specialty. Talk to assistant professors who've had at least three years to become established. Once you get to know them, discuss your questions about the professorial option. Ask their honest assessment of teaching, as well as the research required for tenure.

Many former grad students who opted for a business career felt their lives were in limbo while they were in grad school. In light of the uncertainties, they were reluctant to remain in limbo for another six years. A job in business that only requires 40–50 hours a week, and that can be left behind in the evening and on weekends, sounds like heaven.

In selecting a business path, many former grad students realized they could satisfy their intellectual and scientific interests by independently reading journals and publications. Similarly, they could satisfy their cultural needs with trips to museums and concerts. They concluded that so long as they had a few intellectual companions, they didn't have to be professors. Another reason cited for choosing business was the green factor—money, not environmentalism. Economic considerations can become very important; especially as bills mount and your future plans have no momentum. Although starting salaries in academics are improving, life keeps getting more expensive. It's nice to have a sufficient financial cushion to occasionally indulge in a few luxuries.

Very high-ranking professors can make handsome six-figure salaries, but these are the exceptions. Instead of looking at these numbers in isolation, examine how these figures stack up against the incomes of comparable business positions. The financial rewards for extraordinary business professionals usually contain one or two more zeroes than the salaries of distinguished professors. On campus, it's the football coaches, not the professors, who earn millions of dollars a year.

Beyond the differences in compensation, there are additional financial considerations. In business, you could earn tens of thousands of dollars more than your current income. The income you're giving up during grad school is referred to as an *opportunity cost*. Once you are employed full time, how many years will it take to recoup the money you could have been earning?

If you are paying your own way through school, these numbers can become astronomical. Tuition and fees keep rising. There is an unending list of books and journal subscriptions to purchase. Student loans become a necessity. Although you don't have to pay the money back until you leave school, the interest costs will continue to accumulate every day. These loans will have to be repaid, and normally they cannot be dismissed by filing for bankruptcy

In many disciplines, a multi-year postdoc may be required to gain a tenure-track job. Even if you work exceptionally hard, there are no guarantees you'll get the job you seek. It's depressing to invest so much of your life into a project that may or may not yield results.

Occasionally, you'll be confronted with the sacrifices you're making to follow your dream. When a friend tells you about a big promotion, a vacation in New Zealand, or the purchase of a new home, a business career may look more appealing.

It would be a mistake to believe that everyone in business is making big bucks. On average however, the compensation for comparable positions in business are higher than those of professors. There are many more advancement opportunities in business. Some of these can lead to extremely lucrative compensation. Whether in business or academia, you'll have to work, and work hard, to earn a big salary.

The 800-Pound Gorilla

What are your prospects of being hired as a tenure track professor?
This is a difficult question. The answers can set off emotional alarms that make you want to scream, "I don't want to think about it." It's hard to estimate whether you'll be hired because so many extraneous factors can influence

your chances. It can be difficult to get a precise answer to this question in the best of times. Making a reasonable estimate is even more complex when the job market is in flux. You also have to consider the ranking of your graduate program, your advisor's academic reputation, and the strength of the letter of recommendation he'll write.

University budgets are currently shrinking, and there are fewer openings for new faculty. The shortage of positions is exacerbated because many older professors are postponing their retirement. It was never easy to become an assistant professor—now it's much more competitive.

On the other hand, a few stellar students can feel confident they'll be hired for a tenure-track position. The vast majority of grad students live with uncertainty. There are some other sources of data you could use to determine your academic possibilities. Compare your vitae with those of advanced students who will probably be hired as tenure-track assistant professors.

You could also contact recent graduates who became professors. Ask their perspective on the current job market. If they can review your vitae prior to the discussion, they may be willing to give you a dispassionate estimate of your prospects. Recent grads from your program will have direct experience with the job market. They can give you a realistic perspective.

In addition to talking to your major professor, you can also talk to other professors in the department. It may be challenging to create a climate in which they feel free to give you their honest judgment. No one likes to deliver bad news, so unless your performance has been truly dismal, professors are inclined to paint a cautiously optimistic picture.

When professors make their predictions, listen carefully to their use of any qualifying phrase. They may be trying to protect themselves, as well as you, by veiling a pessimistic estimate. Listen for phrases such as "assuming you are very productive" . . . "if you really strengthen your vitae" . . . "if you can get *all* those papers published."

To increase the chances they'll be completely forthright, you must establish a context for the discussion by making it undeniably clear that you want the truth. Reassure them that if they give you their realistic perspective, you won't have a meltdown in their office, or go on a martini marathon. Alert them ahead of time that you are seeking their advice because you respect their opinion. As you enter their office, reaffirm that you're looking forward to a frank conversation. Explain that you want the truth because you need to make some hard decisions.

The writing may already be on the wall. You may have a good idea of what each professor will say. Prior to these meetings, set your expectations a notch or two below the anticipated conversation. Protect yourself—that way you're less likely to be shocked or disappointed. If a professor does in fact render a pessimistic judgment, don't interrogate them or get defensive. Instead, ask for their suggestions about possible career alternatives.

Sometimes another faculty member (other than your dissertation advisor) will be more honest and direct. Your major professor may have a vested interest in keeping you around for a few more years. They may want your help with research. If you suspect someone may have a conflict of interest, you'll have to temper their encouraging words.

If you receive some bad news about your future in academics, it may take a while to digest. A person's reaction to negative news can be described by the acronym, *SARA*. Initially we experience *Surprise*, and then we often feel *Anger*, followed by *Rejection* or denial, and finally *Acceptance*. The SARA reaction pattern varies from person to person, and from situation to situation. The common thread is that it takes time to heal and move on.

The news that you have a low likelihood of getting a tenure-track job can either be immobilizing or liberating. You may not like the prognosis, but the facts are on the table and now you can begin to move forward. It was inevitable that you'd have to face this reality. By knowing the truth, you can save a great deal of time and money. You can start to focus on other options. And, you can regain control of your life and use this book to chart a new course.

Do You Have Options?

Subtle psychological forces can impact your career decisions. Many graduate students are so committed to becoming professors, they never really think about alternative careers. You begin to think there's no other work that could make you happy. The fact that you think there is only one option can cause you to make that choice seem even more attractive. This is a version of what's called *sour grapes thinking*. It's modeled after Aesop's fable. Once there was a fox who tried many times to jump up and grab a piece of fruit. After repeated failures, he finally walked away convinced he was better off: "The grapes were probably sour anyway." Without your awareness, you may have unconsciously denigrated a business career (because you didn't think you could have it) and artificially elevated your opinion of academia.

A realistic decision depends upon an honest evaluation of all available options. It's important to learn as much as possible about jobs in business, government and nonprofit organizations. The more research and information you gather, the more you'll be able to make an informed decision. An objective examination of the career path you wish to follow will add to your confidence and help you achieve your goal.

4

Town and Gown

"Town and gown" is a well-established catchall phrase for the differences that separate the secular world of business and the "sacred" world of academics. Too often, the inhabitants of each sphere rely on oversimplified dichotomies that exaggerate the contrast. For example, most business people acknowledge that while professors are intelligent, they're unrealistic idealists who aren't fully in touch with the world. Many professors aren't very generous in their assessment of business people and their level of intelligence. Business types tend to be stereotyped as motivated solely by shortsighted self-interest and financial concerns, rather than by the higher values that supposedly guide the actions of academics.

As with most cases of prejudice, it's possible to find instances that partially confirm the stereotype. In truth, the gaps between the two spheres is much smaller than is commonly portrayed. The distinctions are more quantitative than qualitative. Recognizing that the two distribution curves often overlap, here is a summary of comments made by former grad students who transitioned to business.

Worldview

Both academia and business function in their own worlds. Utilizing the metaphor of worlds, the broad boundaries of academic disciplines (e.g., chemistry, linguistics, psychology, history) correspond to different countries. Within each country there are regions that are comparable to a discipline's specialty areas (e.g., social psychology, clinical psychology, neuropsychology, evolutionary psychology), and this usually forms the core of a faculty member's professional identity. Just as regions have metropolitan areas, further sub-disciplines demarcate more specific domains (e.g., military history, intellectual history, social history, etc.). In the same way a citizen reads the local newspaper, professors read the journals and information boards devoted to their subspecialty. They attend professional meetings to discuss the latest ideas with other people who work in their particular area, and to exchange gossip.

People in business use two factors to define their small world: their particular industry (e.g., automotive, finance, technology) and the type of work they perform (e.g., accounting, quality control, human resources, marketing). Like their academic counterparts, business people read publications devoted to their industry and attend conferences and trade shows with other people who toil in the same vineyards. They also enjoy gossip.

Ideas

Ideas are highly prized in academia, especially if the ideas are clever and original. Theories, models, and conceptual frameworks are the currency of serious discourse. Professors frequently have an emotional reaction to aesthetically pleasing ideas. They're favorably disposed to theoretical conceptions with a small number of internally consistent assumptions that explain a wide range of phenomena (e.g., $E = mc^2$). In discussing a theory they sometimes become enthralled by its elegance. Nothing is more valued than an idea that completely challenges the field's dominant paradigm.

Business people encounter many ideas. The challenge they face is weeding out the best idea from the many ideas that come across their desks. Their standards for judging the value of an idea are practical rather than aesthetic. A "good" idea is one that works because it solves a real-world problem and helps create a profit. It doesn't matter that an idea has inconsistencies, is cumbersome, or has been tried by other companies—so long as it works. Business people sometimes marvel at an idea, especially if it significantly impacts the bottom line.

While creative and innovative ideas are highly prized in both academics and business, the criteria for judging the quality of an idea varies. In business, the standard of excellence is determined by whether the idea produces financial results. Pure academicians emphasize a theory's explanatory and predictive power, and leave its practical application to others.

Priorities

The customer is the primary focus of most successful businesses. Customers are important because their purchases pay the bills. Without customers there would be no money to pay salaries and create a profit. Providing the products and services that economically satisfy people's needs is a sure recipe for business success. The principle is so obvious, it's surprising how many companies don't follow it.

Some businesses sell almost exclusively to retail customers, while others (sometimes called OEMs—Original Equipment Manufacturers) sell to businesses. Their transactions are referred to as B2B, or business-to-business sales. A simple example would be a company that provides automotive parts, such as tires, to automotive manufacturers.

The customer is so critical that companies regularly conduct research (this could be a possible job for social science grad students) on customer satisfaction. "Mystery shoppers" are planted to secretly assess a store's level of service. Firms talk about *internal* as well as *external* customers. Internal customers are people within the firm who use the services of another department. For example, the department of human resources provides information on health service benefits to all employees. The goal is to provide the same high level of service to internal as well as external customers.

Which group of people is of greatest concern to professors? Graduate and undergraduate students are a university's primary customers. Their tuition dollars pay salaries and maintain the campus. While most professors care about undergraduates, too often students in large undergraduate classes are treated as lesser citizens. They are taken for granted and don't receive the respect and service they deserve.

The prime concern of many faculty members is the small group of people within their academic subspecialty. Winning the admiration and respect of this network of professional colleagues and graduate students can produce personal benefits. These are the people who can cite your publications, invite you to write a chapter for a book, and vote to support your grant proposal when it comes before a national review panel. In a sense, these disciplinary colleagues are "customers" because their decisions ultimately impact a professor's bottom line.

Numbers

In scientific and scholarly research, numbers are used as a means to an end. Statistical comparisons are used as the basis for judging whether a particular hypothesis can be disconfirmed. Numeric datasets take on significance in relation to particular theories or models. Numbers don't speak for themselves. Their meaning is based on the theoretical context in which they are interpreted. Quantitative analysis is usually a mechanism for evaluating the adequacy of a hypothesis or theoretical explanation.

In business, numbers are virtually an end in and of themselves. This is because numbers are used to measure such critical factors as sales volume, market share, production costs, and operating efficiency—all of which are the basis of a company's profitability. Business people focus on "making their numbers" because these figures represent the difference between success and failure, growth and bankruptcy, and getting a raise or a pink slip. Used descriptively, numeric data tells the story that matters most in business.

Numbers are used to measure performance in both worlds—e.g., the number of research citations in academics, or customer satisfaction ratings in business. In general, these metrics are somewhat more objective in the business world. While professors are concerned about their annual merit review, business people are often held accountable in shorter time frames (e.g., daily output, monthly sales, quarterly results). While a professor's performance is reviewed annually, salary increases are sometimes based on output over a two- or three-year period.

Higher Goals

Professors describe their work as involving the creation, transmission and preservation of knowledge. They see themselves as part of a larger endeavor that transcends time and place. They're building a knowledge base that will be of value to humankind for hundreds of years. From a vantage point removed from daily life, the mission of most professors is to expand human understanding and the aesthetic appreciation of our universe.

Business leaders sometimes discuss the values that are the basis of the company's culture. Occasionally, they'll express a commitment to build a company that stands the test of time. Although they may espouse lofty ideals, their focus is primarily on immediate, short-term results. Long-range thinking is usually done in annual meetings, where strategic plans are formulated for the next one to three years. The economic environment of most businesses can change so suddenly, they must be prepared to dramatically alter their plans. It's not that business people aren't interested in higher values. They just don't commonly think of the workplace as the arena to achieve these goals. Instead, they rely on religious, cultural and community institutions outside business.

Community Involvement

Professors, especially in the humanities, very eloquently express the importance of moral and ethical values in the context of our shared humanity. They convey compassion toward less fortunate people and encourage students to become actively involved in improving the well-being of the community. Students are admonished to perform charitable activities. The motivation for helping is to be based solely on the sense of satisfaction that is intrinsic to charitable activity, and not for reasons of personal gain or self-interest.

Although business people seldom espouse higher moral values, they are often actively involved in service and humanitarian activities within their community. Corporations make massive donations to charitable endeavors. (Universities are often the beneficiaries of this largesse.) Employees of smaller companies often donate their time and resources to fundraising initiatives and community projects. Boards of directors of nonprofit organizations are disproportionately composed of business leaders rather than professors. Many business people become passionately involved in charitable activities through their church, synagogue, or mosque.

While professors may talk about higher values, business people are more likely to put these values into action (i.e., they "walk the talk," in the language of business.). This is due in part to the secondary benefits that result from charitable activities. A company's image is enhanced when it is associated with a charity. Networking with other board members could lead to new business opportunities.

In general, business people are more sociable than academics. At the management level, business is filled with meetings, team activities, and social gatherings. They laugh frequently, and appear to take great enjoyment in life.

Business leaders approach community service in a way that is consistent with their political beliefs. They tend to endorse a political philosophy that emphasizes individual responsibility over collective or government solutions. Yes, business leaders are much more conservative politically than professors—but below the top echelon, you'll find a wide range of opinions. It would be easier to find Democrats at the office than to spot Republicans among the faculty assembly.

Autonomy

This is the arena in which a professor has a great advantage. Once—and this is the big qualifier—you have achieved tenure, there are fewer restrictions and much less stress. Post-tenure faculty members have virtual job security for life. Professors have almost complete independence in selecting their research topics. While there is flexibility in one's research topic, professors are, however, always expected to publish, make professional presentations, and obtain grants.

When it comes to choosing what courses to teach, the content to cover, and how to teach it, professors have great liberty. Deans and department chairs seldom issue directives to faculty members. In business, however, you can expect people higher in the organization to assign your projects. You might collaborate with your boss in a planning discussion, but he or she will make the final decision Former graduate students who now conduct research in a business setting have found it unsettling to be suddenly switched to a different assignment.

The lives of business people are constrained by metrics, benchmark goals, deadlines, and budget constraints (remember the numbers). The performance levels of an individual and of his or her unit are evaluated quarterly, and in some cases daily, weekly, and monthly. Your manager will probably work with you to improve your output.

Time deadlines in business are common, and short. Customers and bosses often expect things to be done immediately. You may have to work overtime and on the weekend. Professors must sometimes meet a specific deadline for an application or publication. The date is almost always announced enough in advance so they can easily incorporate it in their schedule.

Teamwork

Teamwork, information sharing, and effective communication are hallmarks of successful business people. The complexity of products and services require employees from different parts of the company to coordinate their activities. For example, one group will design a new product, other people will manufacture it, while still others will ship it. A separate department is responsible for sales. A group of accountants then keeps track of the expenses and income. Groups of people from design, manufacturing, shipping, sales, etc., will meet in what are referred to as cross-functional teams to orchestrate everyone's actions.

While cross-disciplinary research is lauded, most professors operate alone. In this sense, each professor is an entrepreneur who creates his or her own business. Professors set their research agenda, and generate grant money to support the work. Within any professor's laboratory or research group, there is a general culture of cooperation. An undercurrent of competition flows beneath the surface ("What will be the order of authorship on this paper?"). A new grad student may initially work on an older student's research, but the expectation is that sooner or later—and preferably sooner—everyone will be doing their own studies.

This is not to suggest that business is a wonderland of cooperation, free of competition. There is an abundance of competition, especially with competing firms. There is also competition between units and between individuals within those units.

Power and Influence

As every grad student quickly learns, your major professor has an amazing amount of influence over your career. Many professors create their own fiefdoms. As the principal investigator who obtained the research grant, the professor has broad discretionary power and influence over the people who are funded by this grant. Professors also have sweeping authority within a classroom. They can issue edicts about the subject matter and dates of exams. Since professors operate within such small boundaries, many do not develop the "softer" skills of influencing people.

The same positional power also exists in business. In some management structures, however, the decision-making authority can be diffused. For example, project teams often cut across functional lines. While within the team, no one person is appointed as the ultimate decision maker. Because there's no formal designation of authority in these teams, individuals must become highly skilled at persuasion and negotiation to get things done. If you've ever been in a class with a lab group, or been part of an informal study group, you're familiar with how problematic it can be to get everyone to pull their share of the work. Individuals with these soft interpersonal skills are often recognized as having leadership abilities. Consequently they're often the first to be promoted to a position of greater responsibility.

Compensation

The distribution curve for salaries in both academics and business are bell shaped. The mean is somewhat higher in the for-profit world, and the upper end of the curve extends much longer. People work very hard in business, and they are well paid in return. A related advantage in business is the greater number of opportunities for advancement. When a business is expanding, whether it is large or small, there will be many new job openings. Most companies have a "hire from within" policy that gives preference to current employees.

Most professors are relatively immobile, and only make one or two moves in a lifetime. Business people are regularly transferred to different locations and jobs. They may also change companies several times in their careers. All these changes create opportunities to improve both your position and compensation.

Each world has a distinctive culture. Weigh the advantages and disadvantages of each when making your career choice.

5

What Are Your Interests?

When you've been dreaming about a life in academia, it's hard to imagine the business world could ever be as satisfying. No alternative career seems to compare. Any other job might feel as though you're settling for less. The fact is, business jobs are just as challenging and rewarding. The difference between A and B isn't as large as you might imagine.

There are many hybrid jobs in the grey zone between the worlds of A and B. For example, the non-professorial jobs inside universities and colleges have many parallels with business. University employees who recruit high school students are similar to job recruiters, and people counseling students are analogous to career counselors in business.

Would you be willing to consider one of these hybrid jobs? Or, do you reject any career except becoming an academician? Exploring the full range of jobs in the grey area between the two poles requires a degree of open-mindedness. A good starting point is a story that illuminates a critical business skill—negotiation.

A disagreement between two sisters is described in *Getting to Yes*, the classic book about negotiation based on the Harvard Negotiation Project. Two sisters are in conflict over the only orange in the house. After listening to the squabble for several minutes, a wise parent intercedes.

Both of the young women indicate they want the orange for a recipe. The mother asks Anna why she needs the orange, and she responds, "I need the juice for a smoothie." Barbara, the other sister, explains she needs the orange peel to make zest for her muffins.

While oversimplified, the story illustrates the conceptual distinction between a person's *position* and their *interests*. A *position* is what you think you need in order to achieve your goals. Each girl's position is that she wants the orange. *Interests* are the goals your position will enable you to achieve. Anna's interest is to make a smoothie, and Barbara's is to bake muffins. A *position* is what you want, and *interests* are the reasons you want it. Like the sisters, many individuals become adamant when they fall into the trap of thinking *only* one position can make them happy.

The positions of two sisters may be in conflict, but not necessarily their interests. Although each daughter wants the orange, Anna only needs the juice, and Barbara wants the peel to grate for zest. Many students have an unwavering position. They want to be a tenure-track professor. They believe this is the only career that will enable them to attain their long-term *interest* of living a life that is both significant and stimulating. The practical question becomes: Is being a professor the *only* thing that can satisfy your interests?

No doubt, there are other careers that might result in a meaningful life. By clarifying your interests and modifying your position, you may discover an alternative career path. This approach won't pinpoint an ideal job, but it will help expand your career horizons.

Have you carefully outlined your interests? What personal goals will a career in academia enable you to achieve? Are you drawn to teaching? Does research have the greatest appeal? And, what is it about teaching and research that you find attractive?

If teaching tops your list, could you be happy teaching a subject other than geology, anthropology, or history? If so, your interest (teaching) might be attained in more ways than through your position as a professor. Is your interest in teaching limited to college-age students? You might also enjoy teaching adults or children. There are many opportunities to teach adults within the corporate world. Government agencies and not-for-profit organizations also conduct a range of educational programs. You may also find satisfaction teaching grades K–12.

Which of your talents and abilities is employed when you teach? Do you enjoy using your analytic ability to organize and structure course content? Are your creative talents exercised when you make complex concepts understandable? Do you have a distinctive skill for communicating information? Do you like the challenge of thinking on your feet to answer a student's questions? Teaching a large class involves a great deal of management. Perhaps your management ability could be considered another asset. Using one or more of these skills may become your prime interest.

For example, some professors are most comfortable doing one-on-one tutoring. Their satisfaction is based on coaching and advising individuals. Tens of thousands of people work as "executive coaches." They coach managers and executives on how to become more effective leaders. Perhaps you're good with people. Teaching is only one arena where you can use these skills. You might want to work with customers or become a manager in an organization.

In analyzing the reasons you like teaching, you may realize your interest is in finding work that enables you to use and develop these skills. This knowledge will allow you to identify other careers where you might utilize these abilities.

The same analysis can be applied to your interests in research. Do you enjoy the conceptual and creative thinking required to formulate hypotheses and interpret results? Do you find pleasure in the process of conducting studies? Communicating research results may suit your special interests. Or, do you like keeping up-to-date with the latest findings in your discipline, regardless of whether you have conducted the research?

Problem-solvers are always in demand. Creativity and innovation always top the list of attributes most desired in employees. You might use your communication skills to share research findings with experts in other disciplines, or with the general public. The knowledge and skills of research scientists are needed to evaluate patent applications in the life sciences. Can your imagination take you beyond the position "Professor Smith or nothing," to envision other possibilities?

If the campus environment interests you, you could apply for a staff position at a university. The number of non-academic staff positions almost equals the number of professors. Academically inclined grad students might work in the office of the provost, dean, or even the graduate school. If you enjoy working with students, you might consider student services (organizing activities and clubs), or advising students on class selection and career plans. You can readily investigate the range of business jobs that exist on campus by talking to people who hold these positions.

Colleges and universities provide many cultural and intellectual riches. But these same resources are available outside the walls of academics. Distinguished people regularly give public presentations. High-quality art exhibits and musical performances are readily accessible. Most major cities have excellent bookstores. All this may be more convenient on campus, but you could easily participate in these activities while working in business.

Many of the people you see at public classical music concerts, in art museums, public lectures, and Barnes & Noble, work in business. These people have abiding intellectual interests. That's why they avidly read the *New York Times* science section on Tuesday, and the book reviews on Sunday. You don't have to work on campus to satisfy your interest in art, literature, and science.

One exciting line of work falls under many headings (e.g., university development, development, fundraising, or alumni relations). Raising monetary donations is a necessity in any college or university. Combining your people skills with your disciplinary knowledge could qualify you for this type of job.

To investigate other career possibilities on campus, you might find a part-time job in administration. This would provide a good introduction to on-campus work. Hands-on experience is essential in determining whether this type of work is a good fit with your interests.

Loss

This chapter has highlighted the many ways you might be satisfied in a non-academic career. Working in business, however, will never be exactly the same as working in academia. You will be giving up some lifestyle benefits. Adjusting to this kind of loss is an emotional process that can take time. While each person's grief is unique, everyone goes through a period of adjustment.

Some people submerge themselves in negative feelings. They go through intense outpourings of tears, anger, self-pity, and self-condemnation. Others move into denial and thereby avoid their sense of loss. Once they have established a new life, they're more likely to examine these feelings. Regardless of your approach, it is important to acknowledge your emotions. It's honest and constructive to admit your myriad of feelings. You'll be able to learn more from the experience, and you'll be more empathetic with others who are wrestling with the same transition.

Settling for More or Less

What are some of the worst losses you might imagine in your life? How would you be affected by a debilitating injury or a life threatening illness? In his book *Stumbling on Happiness,* Daniel Gilbert summarizes many studies on loss. In his research, Professor Gilbert compares the predictions of healthy people about how they think they would react to such calamities with the reactions of people who actually suffered such events.

These extreme events seem so horrific that many of us can't even fathom how we'd survive. Healthy people often predict they would be very unhappy and depressed if they became gravely ill. In reality, most people cope amazingly well, following an initial period of adjustment. Each of us has a "set point" for our personal happiness. People with average happiness before a tragedy return to average happiness after an event; people who were not very happy before remain the same; and people who were relatively high on the happiness scale are able to continue to find great pleasure in life.

The mere idea of changing careers can seem like a devastating blow to some grad students. Like the participants in Gilbert's studies, they can't imagine being satisfied with any non-academic career. Former grad students, however, experienced a complete change of perspective after successfully transitioning to business. In retrospect, they realized their conception of academia was idealized. Their dream overlooked some of the unpleasant parts of the job. In contrast, they imagined business as mostly negative. When they eventually moved into business, they realized their new career was much more stimulating and sophisticated than they had imagined.

Ultimately, there is only one way to find out if you're suited for a career in business. You must try it. In Chapter 12, you'll learn ways to test the waters by volunteering or working part-time. As you define your interests and discover alternative ways to use your strengths, you'll realize that far from settling, you can in fact satisfy your interests.

6

Why B?

Can you imagine yourself in this scenario? Throughout your school years you've shared an apartment with various roommates. In late spring, you and a friend find a spacious apartment for next year. The day before you're scheduled to sign the lease, your friend backs out of the deal. You're very disappointed— but as luck would have it, your favorite cousin is looking for a roommate. Even though your problem has been solved, you ask your friend why he changed his mind.

His explanation could prove very significant for the future of your friendship. If he says he "just felt like it," you might see him as untrustworthy and unreliable. If he claims to have found someone else to live with, you may infer that he doesn't like you, and you may want to rethink the friendship. If, however, he says he just can't swing the rent and will be moving in with his parents, you'll most likely wish him well and remain friends.

Our curiosity is naturally piqued when there is a drastic change in the plans or commitments of the people we care about. The more significant the relationship, the more questions we're likely to have. You want to know why a friend is leaving a romantic relationship, or why a colleague didn't go to her father's funeral. The explanations people give for their actions can alter our opinion of them forever.

When you make the transition from A to B, your academic colleagues, your future business associates, your loved ones and friends, will be extremely interested in your reasons. At times you might be tempted to say, "It's none of your business," but that's hardly appropriate. You'll need to craft a well-thought-out explanation.

What To Say

The most effective explanation is honest, plausible, concise, and positive. Your answer should be sufficiently detailed to address most, but not necessarily every, question. When you're talking with colleagues in academia, you should focus on the unique benefits of business rather than the limitations of academia.

There are no pat answers, since every student's situation is unique. Everyone needs to use words and phrases that feel natural. Here are some examples that will inspire you to create your own explanations. "After a great deal of thought, I've decided to look into a business career. As much as I enjoy academic research and theories, I've become more interested in real-world applications."

You can elaborate on this theme by talking about how you've changed: "As a result of my grad school classes and research, I've discovered that I love putting ideas into practice. I receive the greatest satisfaction from work that has a direct impact on people's lives. Therefore, I'm looking for a profession that more closely fits these goals."

Your explanation will be more compelling if you include a short anecdote about an incident that prompted your decision: "One day after a seminar, I realized that all the ideas I was generating were about real-life applications rather than research questions." Another approach is to link your explanation to your family: "The day my daughter asked for an ice cream and I had to tell her we couldn't afford it, I vowed I wasn't going to continue living on the borderline of poverty." Personal epiphanies can be overly dramatic, but they communicate sincerity: "After my father passed away I realized I was in graduate school to please him. My passion lies outside the university."

You could also discuss your life goals and how they've shifted: "As I observed my professors, I realized the academic life was not for me. I'm not ready to make this kind of commitment. When I considered what it would take to earn tenure, I concluded I want time for other things in my life."

It's important to indicate that you didn't arrive at your decision in haste. By emphasizing how serious you are about this new direction, people will be much less likely to try to talk you out of it. Instead, they'll say things such as: "It sounds as though you have already made up your mind. Please know that I wish you well."

Two or three sentences will be sufficient to explain your decision, especially if the tone of your voice and facial expression communicates your sincerity. Be prepared for people to suggest their own explanation for your decision (some of which may not be flattering), or to ask probing questions. Vague explanations, such as the following, will automatically stimulate more questions:

"I just decided I don't want to be a professor."
"Business feels like a better fit for me."
"Business suits my lifestyle."

Instead, give one specific reason, and then move on to describe the alternative career paths you're considering. Your goal is to refocus the discussion on your future, not your past.

Friends and Key Professors

Why do you feel more comfortable around some people than others? A key factor is that you know how they're likely to act. The same is true for people who care about you. When you do something out of the ordinary, people begin to wonder if they really understand you. ("I can't believe Frances would make such a change. I thought I knew her.") A radical change in your plans can be disconcerting to people. They may even feel some uncertainty and fear.

You may want to go into more detail with your close family and friends. List the pros and cons, and explain how you arrived at your decision. Some people may have trouble accepting your choice. They may even quote some of your prior statements about the glories of academics and the horrors of business. Although they are raising questions about the wisdom of your choice, ultimately they are on your side and they'll support you. Your decision will not come as a complete surprise if you discussed the choice with them before making a final commitment.

After sharing your plans with friends and family, it's time to see your major professor. This could be the most daunting person you'll have to face, especially if he or she doesn't have an inkling about your interest in business. Don't put off this meeting; it will only work to your disadvantage. You want your professor to hear your decision directly from you, not from a secondhand source. Schedule an appointment ASAP.

If your major professor regards you as a potential shining academic star, as well as a research colleague, you'll probably receive a great deal of resistance to your announcement. The best way to avoid this reaction is to speak with clarity and confidence (i.e., practice giving your explanation). Start by praising your professor and the grad program. Next, lay out the reasons behind your decision. Be prepared for lots of questions and some serious disagreement.

"You're making a mistake." You may have heard this comment from friends, but your major professor may use it to launch into an overwhelming list of reasons why you should stay in school. While it's useful to plan your response to such a confrontation, listen carefully and consider all the arguments. It's possible that you'll learn new information or gain a different perspective. You may even want to reconsider your decision.

If the discussion gets lengthy, tense, or confusing, take a time-out. It isn't necessary to resolve everything at this initial meeting. (Don't be shocked by the possible accusations that you're selling out or abandoning your principles.) You always have the prerogative of requesting additional time to consider the points that have been raised. Ask to revisit the discussion in the near future. Take a few days to reframe your thinking and refocus your arguments.

The time interval will give you both a chance to dispassionately reconsider your positions. Remember the SARA model of how people react to unexpected information: surprise; anger; resignation; and acceptance. With the passage of a few days, your major professor may be able to stand back and be more objective about your decision. Prepare your remarks before the next meeting. This is an important discussion—don't hesitate to take notes along. While you may be prepared for a more contentious debate, you may be surprised to find your advisor's stance has softened or changed completely.

Professors invest a great deal of time and psychological energy in training their select graduate students. If you are one of these students, your decision could have significant negative consequences for your advisor. Your departure means you will not be available to assist in research. You may have been spotted as one of the future stars he's grooming for a tenure-track job at a major university. This would have elevated your professor's status with colleagues in the department, and in the field. Ultimately, you must do what is right for you, not what would be best for your professor. Even so, it's important to consider the impact of your choice on the interests of your major professor. Be empathetic to his reaction.

Avoid criticizing both your major professor and the graduate program, even if you have good reasons to do so. You may want to call on this professor in the future. Even though you may not give this professor's name as a reference, a diligent interviewer may take the initiative to contact him for "background" information. Save any strong negative feelings about your grad school experience until well after you've landed a job.

If, over the years, your major professor has been less than encouraging about your academic potential, this meeting could be easier than you imagined. As they smile and ask about your timeline, you may get the feeling they're already making plans to re-assign your office space.

You should also make appointments with other faculty members with whom you have a relationship. While they may initially express disappointment or surprise, they'll quickly get on board with your decision. They might even reveal their own interest in business.

Explanations in Business

When business people learn about your educational credentials, they'll be very interested to know why you're abandoning your academic career. Their concerns are largely practical and are most likely centered on issues of your potential "commitment" to business. Your decision raises concerns because the company is about to spend a great deal of time and money to train you. They want to be certain you'll stick with the job and justify their investment.

Interviewers

Always start your explanation by emphasizing your desire to be in the business world. You can discuss the limitations of academia, but temper your remarks. The interviewer may be married to a professor. Talk about the appeal of business rather than hammering away at the negatives of academics. "I want a job that deals directly with real-world challenges. Action is more important to me than theories and debate. I enjoy the process of finding ways to translate ideas into practical results."

Innovation is highly valued in the business world, so try and work this theme into the conversation. "I understand the importance of research, but I find it somewhat repetitive. I'm more interested in creating innovative ideas and working across boundaries to turn them into practical results."

Are you a risk-taker? This trait is highly prized in business. Without sounding reckless, emphasize that you possess this quality. "I like to explore new options rather than doing minor variations on the same idea. I'm willing to take *reasonable* risks, if they'll yield substantial benefits."

If you take pride in your interpersonal skills, stress that you want to work in a job where you can use these abilities. "I like working directly with people. It gives me great pleasure to know I helped a team achieve its goal." Or, "I'm good at writing and speaking. I wanted to communicate to a broader audience outside academics. I hope to use my talents to communicate ideas that have a real-world impact."

When you offer these explanations in a job interview, you'll need to be ready to document these statements. In later chapters you'll learn to prepare concrete examples that demonstrate the validity of the attributes (e.g., practical, innovative, team player, good communicator) you claim to possess.

Your goal in every interview is to make it irrefutably clear—you are 100% committed to a career in business. Never qualify your interest in business. If you say, "I thought I'd give this a try and see if I like it," your job prospects will immediately drop to zero.

Ironically, you can use your years of graduate study as a way to convince an interviewer that you never intend to go back to academics. "I believe knowing what you *don't* want to do can be as valuable as knowing what you want. I gave academics my full commitment for three years, and I'm absolutely certain it's not for me. I'm eager to start the rest of my life."

Students who never seriously considered becoming a professor have a ready explanation. "I went to school to for the training in analytic thinking and to develop research skills. Now that I have these skills, I'm ready to apply them in business." You can use this explanation in almost any job interview, but it's especially applicable to a job in research.

Business Contacts

After you're hired, the people you work with will want to know about your past. If they learn you were in grad school, they'll most likely ask why you didn't become a professor. You can briefly acknowledge that you attended grad school, and then give your job interview explanation. Some business people have reservations about academicians, so the best approach is to keep your answers short.

After you offer an explanation, gracefully change the subject by asking about their career path:

"How long have you been with the company?"
"Why did you decide to go into this business?"
"Where do you see yourself in the next 5 to 10 years?"

A common mistake made by many grad students at the beginning of their business careers is to make frequent references to their good old days in grad school, or to reminisce about former professors. In a business meeting they may preface their remarks with such phrases as:

"The latest empirical research shows . . . ."
"The preponderance of studies on this topic supports the idea that . . ."
"As Professor X at Harvard used to say. . ."

Instead of elevating your credibility, you'll quickly become known as "the professor," and it won't be a compliment.

Without naming faculty members, citing a specific journal, or, worst of all,
quoting from your master's thesis, you can make your point by alluding to a
person you knew in the past, or an article you once read. Such oblique references won't draw attention to your academic background. Let your ideas stand
on their own. You don't have to back them up with footnotes.

When you meet business people outside your company, there is no need to
volunteer details about your work history. If you believe someone might be a
future resource, you can save the conversation about your past for later.

You'll need scripted answers to questions that might arise about your move
from the academic to the business world. Use the examples in this chapter as a
starting point. Your own explanation will emerge as you talk with more and
more people. If you rehearse in private before going public, you'll be able to
deliver your answers with confidence. Soon, you'll be able to move the discussion away from yourself and get back to business.

Entering the Business World

7

Your Career Trajectory

Landing a job is similar to catching fish. There are two common approaches to fishing. You can identify the kind of fish you want, and then bait a hook with its favorite food. Or, you can you drag a net through the water, haul up many different fish, and decide which ones to keep and which to throw back. In a metaphoric sense, you're fishing for a job. Which strategy will you use?

Targeted Job Search

How specific can you be about the type of work you're seeking? Instead of saying "I want to do research," can you zero in on a certain type of research? Are you able to identify the industry in which you'd like to be employed? Do you have the name of a company? The more precisely you can identify the target, the easier it will be to prepare and search a job.

You undoubtedly used this approach when preparing for an academic career. You knew you wanted to become a professor, and that to qualify you needed a Ph.D. You identified the academic discipline and the subspecialty. You then applied to graduate schools that had a program tailored to your interests.

A small percentage of people seem to know, even from an early age, exactly what kind of job they want. Whether it's based on experience, family influence, or intuition, they believe there is only one profession for them. In career advice books, this is called having a passion or a dream. The phrase "follow your bliss" is used to poetically capture this approach to seeking your life's work.

Some career advisors imply you should only take a job that aligns with your inner passion.

Individuals who have a clear picture of their target can tailor their job search to a specific industry and to a particular type of work. They know which publications to read and where to look for job postings. They focus on building a network by meeting people in the field. In job interviews, their commitment to the profession subtly infuses their answers to questions.

If you are one of these people, you can jump to the next section. Here's a word of caution before you skip ahead. It's surprising how many people who "followed their bliss" became dissatisfied after a few years on the job.

Good, Better, then Best Job

The vast majority of people are unsure *exactly* what kind of work would be most satisfying. They engage in a more generalized job search before selecting a career. Most people consider many different career possibilities and then narrow their alternatives. Like fishing with a net, most of us don't know exactly what we want until we see and touch it. Lacking a clear definition of the target makes it difficult to know where to look, or what kind of job to seek. It's almost as blind as closing your eyes and throwing a dart at a map. "Ah, South Dakota, that's where we'll take our vacation."

Clearly, your job search strategy is more informed than throwing darts. You'll begin by researching several industries and career fields in which you'd like to work. Then, you'll use that knowledge to narrow your focus to starter jobs in a few industries.

Your first job doesn't have to be the perfect job. Most likely it will not be aligned with your "bliss." That will come later, in subsequent jobs. The job doesn't have to be with a well known Fortune 500 corporation. Your goal is to find a good starter job, not necessarily a great job. The attributes of a good job will be defined shortly, but one of the key features is opportunity; both to learn and to advance.

Once you have a good job, you can further evaluate your options and how you move from this good job to a better one. It could be a better job in your company, or a switch to a different company and industry. In this next job, you can repeat the evaluation process to further refine your definition of a great job. The good-better-best strategy may take several years, and may involve more than two job changes before you move from good to great.

This approach can be used to attain any life goal. It's variously referred to as successive approximations, triangulation, bootstrapping, or "one step at a time." You start the journey even though you don't know exactly where you're going. Once you're on the path, you'll develop a better sense of where you want to go and how to get there.

You can begin to narrow the focus of your job search by researching several industries in which you might work, and the kind of work you're qualified for. Chapter 8 provides guidance on the narrowing process. Basically, you want to identify four or five industries that sound interesting (e.g., travel, health care, education, pharmaceuticals). Next, select a few functional areas in which you are prepared to work (e.g., human resources, research, communication, sales).

Only after becoming established in this "good" job will you be able to decide if it is an area that is your life's calling. If it is, you may want to do more research to identify the companies with the best growth potential. It may take only one more change to align your work with your heart.

A basic rule of the job search process is that it's easier to get a job if you already *have* a job. It's also easier to move from one functional area to another within the same organization. Since you will have established an outstanding performance record, you'll be more qualified to move to a better job. Plus, you've had time to build connections inside the company.

Here's how the good–better–best strategy worked for several individuals without a Ph.D., and for one who had the degree.

After her first year of grad school, Betina realized academia was not her forte. To pay living expenses, she took a receptionist job at the U.S. headquarters of a major Japanese automotive company. She was amazed at the amount of competition for this relatively low-level position. It didn't take long to understand why. The company was growing, and they treated their employees exceptionally well. Although she knew she was capable of much more, she excelled at her position and concentrated on learning about the company. After some research, she realized she wanted to work in corporate and dealer education. When she saw an opening for a receptionist in the Learning Center, she applied and was hired. During the next year she observed the instructors in the general management skills courses. Her next goal was to become an instructor herself.

Betina studied the lesson plans and practiced her delivery. When an instructor's slot opened, she begged for a chance to interview. People were amazed at her knowledge and teaching skills. She was hired. Because she was so exceptional, in two years she moved up to the position of lead trainer. Along the way, she met other successful trainers from around the country. Many of them were well-paid freelancers who were hired on a contract basis by all of the major foreign and domestic automotive corporations. Now she had a new goal.

She finally mustered the courage to start her own training company. Ironically, the first firm that hired her was the corporation where she began.

While pursing a degree in the social sciences, Ricardo became very adept at survey research. He decided to leave grad school after his third year and take a research position with the federal government. It was easy to move from job to job inside the government. He quickly moved to a position with a different agency in Washington, D.C. Because he was working at the center of the federal government, he discovered many new opportunities. By now he was a manager, and on the fast track at another agency. From there, he moved to the private sector as an executive at a major healthcare company.

Adam's Ph.D. was in the life sciences, but he decided against becoming a professor. He found a research job at a biotech start-up firm. The firm never became successful, so after two years he changed to a better-paying job with a larger company. Within a year, he moved up to a management position. Realizing his interests had shifted, he began networking with people in marketing. Although it took over a year, he landed an internal job in marketing. As he expected, he loved this work and more promotions followed.

While working on a Ph.D. in the history of science, Devendra got a part-time job as an undergraduate advisor to premed students. He then moved to a better job doing similar work in the School of Engineering. Because of his experience as a career advisor, he was hired by a for-profit firm that helped corporations locate electrical engineers.

Dev essentially worked as a "headhunter." He discovered the best candidates and tried to entice them to leave their current jobs. In this work, he interfaced with human resources departments in different companies. He found it very stressful to work on commission. Dev decided he wanted a salaried job with normal working hours. He was able to switch roles when he was hired by a technology company. He was very happy to work in their HR department and deal with headhunters.

What Is a Good Job?

The good-better-best strategy frees you from the impossible challenge of loving your very first job. Your first job should help you discover your long-term goals. At this point in your career, the ideal job is one that allows you to learn and grow.

Learning is one of your strengths, and once you're in your new job, you'll have a great deal to assimilate. You'll want to expand your knowledge of: business and business people, your company and industry, and yourself.

From the first day at work you'll learn how businesses operate and how they're interconnected. Make it a point to understand the mindset of the people in your new world. Continually seek answers to questions such as:

How do business people think?
What motivates them?
What is important to them?
How do people blend self-interest and the company's interests?
How do they balance their work and personal lives?
What kind of people get ahead, and how do they do it?
Which individuals have power, and how do they use it?

In addition to watching and observing your colleagues, spend time over lunch and after hours expanding your understanding of this new world.

You can learn about business in almost any job. One grad student got an internship in the athletic ticket office on campus. She was surprised by how the employees regarded the students, alumni, and supporters who attended sporting events. They were treated like honored customers, who were deciding how to spend their "entertainment dollars." To increase ticket revenues, it was essential to provide excellent customer service. She watched how these university employees went out of their way to make it easy and enjoyable for people to purchase tickets.

Whether you work for a small firm or a large corporation, you can gain a tremendous amount of information. Work on answering questions such as:

Does your company have a strategy, and how is it being implemented?
Who are its chief competitors, and how does the company deal with them?
What are the company's weaknesses?
Which products are most profitable, and which are least profitable?
Which departments are most favored and why?
Which departments have the least stature and why?
How can you move up within the company?
How would you describe the culture of the company?
What departments could offer the best opportunities for promotion?

Your company operates as one of many in a particular industry. You therefore must understand this world. There's a good chance your next job will probably be with another firm within this sector. Talk with longtime employees and learn the history of this part of the economy. Discover how the major firms achieved prominence. How do they compete against one another? Is the industry subject to economic cycles, and what phase is it in now? You can read current business publications for expert's predictions about its potential long-term growth. It's also useful to understand the differences in the roles of specific functional areas in companies. In some firms, finance may be more important, while the sales department may be more influential in another.

The most important person to observe is *you*. Watch how you deal with the challenges of the first weeks and months on the job. How did people help or hinder your adaptation to the new job?

What do you like about your job, and what doesn't appeal to you?
Which of your characteristics and abilities are most valuable?
What skills do you need to develop?
What situations make you feel most comfortable?
Which situations are the most stressful?
What kind of boss do you like best, and whom do you want to emulate?
What gives you the greatest satisfaction at work?
How important is money?

By gaining a better picture of your personal characteristics, you'll be able to assess your next career move. Are you happy working in business, or would you like to go back to academics? Perhaps you're now qualified for a hybrid job at a university. Do you want to stay with this firm, or find another? What job do you want next? Ask people for their opinions. Their answers will offer new insights into your future. When your boss conducts a review of your performance, ask her about your career path within the organization.

Gathering all this information will help expand your network. Just as people were crucial to getting your first job, they will be the most important factor in locating your next position. Whether or not you plan to stay in your current company, industry, or type of work, you'll need connections to help you move ahead. Build as many relationships as possible, even with people who may never become friends. If you do come into conflict with a colleague, remember—you don't have to be disagreeable when you disagree. Don't pick fights or burn bridges.

The good-better-best strategy is designed for people who do not have an abiding passion about a specific type of work. People with an intense passion for a particular field can use a truncated version of this strategy. Although your first job may be very satisfying, you can still aim for one that is slightly better.

Experience plus knowledge causes most people to redefine the kind of work they truly want to do. As a result, they're always on the lookout for something better. If your desires don't instigate a job switch, then an economic upheaval, a merger, or a complete change in our company's management might force you to look for another position. Regardless of the reason, if you persist and remain open to new possibilities, you'll create your good–better–best future.

8

Industry and Function

You've made the decision to change from A to B. Now you have two more important decisions. What industry do you want to work in? And, what kind of work do you want to do? Understanding the meaning of two concepts—*industry* and *function*—is a good place to start.

Industries

The word *industry* is a hangover from the industrial age, and brings to mind images of steel manufacturing and mining. As you can see below, there are many diverse "industries" or sectors. Each one contains a complex network of related companies. The business world is enormous, and its sectors and subdivisions are comparable to those in academics. Each school within a university is comparable to an industry, and the departments and specialty programs are similar to *sub-sectors*. Here are some of the major industries in the business world:

Accounting	Aerospace & Defense	Agriculture
Automotive	Biotechnology	Chemicals
Communications	Construction	Consulting
Education	Electronics	Energy
Entertainment	Environment	Financial Services
Food & Beverage	Health Care	Hospitality

Industrial Goods	Insurance	Internet
Law	Media	Medical Devices
Mining	Pharmaceuticals	Retail
Real Estate	Safety	Security
Transportation	Travel	Utilities

There are many sub-sector companies within each industry. For example, the healthcare industry also includes hospitals, nursing homes, private medical practices, therapeutic clinics, and testing laboratories. Sometimes the boundaries are blurred. Portions of the pharmaceutical industry overlap with health care.

The automotive industry is an easy example. There are several major auto manufacturers, and then there are the companies which supply the parts used to assemble the car (e.g., tires, wheels, lights, radios, etc.). Other firms supply the equipment and robotic machines for manufacturing. One sub-sector deals in "aftermarket products," which are the gadgets, parts, and ornaments (e.g., fuzzy dice) that people purchase to enhance their cars. There are also the auto repair companies. It's easy to see how each industry consists of a varied and complex network of related companies.

Stock market analysts use the word *sector* instead of industry. These analysts discuss the future growth possibilities within a whole market sector before recommending particular companies. When these commentators refer to a sector, they mean most of the companies within an industry. Some mutual funds are set up as "sector funds," and they only include stocks within one industry (e.g., energy). Instead of estimating which company will do well, you're betting an overall industry or sector will prosper.

The sector in which you work will become an important aspect of how you'll define yourself. Business people use their industry as the foundation for their self-identity (i.e., aerospace, communications, real estate, or utilities). Professors are in the education sector and they're in the higher education sub-segment. The word *professor* also connotes their function, or the type of work they perform.

Each academic discipline has a professional association, just as *trade groups* develop within a business sector. The business equivalent of an annual academic conference is known as a trade show. Entire sectors and sub-sectors will meet on a national and international basis. Both the annual World of Concrete conclave and the Consumer Electronics Show book almost every hotel in Las Vegas for their trade shows. At academic meetings, professors and graduate students use papers to display their latest scholarly output. In the same manner, businesses construct elaborate displays to highlight their latest products and services.

Every company operates in a sector, and by working in a company, you thereby commit to both the company and the sector. This is an important consideration. When you scout possible companies, always connect them with their industry. You'll want to seriously research industries to make your career decisions. The depth of your understanding will cast you in a favorable light during job interviews.

Deciding upon an industry is difficult, because no matter how much research you do, you can only have a limited understanding of the real world you're about to enter. Some industries may be better aligned with your field of study, your skills, and talents. Your personal inclinations are another factor to consider in making your selection. Some people tinker with cars, others are fascinated by computers, and still others are wine connoisseurs.

People are drawn to some industries for the possible side benefits. As you might guess, the travel industry is very popular. Hospitality (hotels, resorts, etc.) can also be very alluring. Since large hotel chains often have properties throughout the world, aspiring hoteliers imagine moving from one exotic locale to another. In a similar manner, the intellectual environment associated with universities is a major benefit of the education industry.

Another important consideration is the economic forecast for each industry. The better its growth potential, the larger the number of advancement opportunities. In terms of your long-term career, it makes sense to select a field that is growing rather than one that's in decline. Within the media sector, newspapers are currently downsizing. Unless there is a drastic change in their business model (i.e., traditionally, they made money from ads, especially classified ads; the rise of the internet and Craigslist has decimated that income stream), recovery and growth are unlikely. By contrast, health care is a growth industry. Since the elderly are the largest consumers of medical services, aging baby boomers are a major component of this growth.

Your career success will be linked to your understanding of, and commitment to, your industry. Salespeople capture this wisdom with phrases such as "know the territory," or "know the customer." This knowledge grows from years of experience and study. People who remain in one industry usually have better opportunities for advancement.

Given the importance of choosing the right industry, you should begin your search by identifying five or six areas of interest. As you learn more about each one, your focus will narrow to two or three. These are the areas in which you will concentrate your job search. Just because you finally make an educated choice, this doesn't seal your fate forever. You can change industries early in your career. Most people jump from one to another at least once, and make even more changes within their chosen occupation.

Functions or Occupations

Many terms are used to describe the variety of work options, such as *occupation, function, career track,* and *profession.* These words are used interchangeably to refer to the kind of work a person performs. Here are some common examples.

Accounting	Administration	Education
Finance	Human Resources	Information Systems
Law	Logistics/Transportation	Management
Maintenance	Marketing	Operations/Production
Purchasing	Research/Design	Sales

Every company in every industry needs people to perform the sales function. To make a profit, companies need to sell their products and services to customers. Retail customers are the most familiar, but often a company's customers are other businesses. When technology companies sell a large order to corporate customers, a whole team of salespeople might interact with a team from the customer's purchasing department. In retail sales, selling is usually a one-to-one relationship.

People in sales and marketing also play an important role in nonprofit organizations. For example, representatives from universities visit high schools to recruit undergraduate applicants. In charitable organizations, the job of convincing people to donate money is similar to selling a company's products.

Large organizations employ many people in each work function. A trip to one of the administrative departments on campus (e.g., human resources, purchasing, or maintenance) will help you understand how people in different functional areas operate inside a university. Some corporations have separate operating companies or units within their larger corporate structure. A parallel would be the athletics department within a university. At large schools, athletics employ individuals in most major occupations.

Organizations work most efficiently when the functional areas effectively communicate and coordinate their activities. For example, the department responsible for designing a new product must coordinate with the operations or production department. Purchasing has to work with operations on what materials to buy. The people in marketing must understand the product months in advance, so they can plan the advertising campaign and distribution strategy. Because operations may need to increase its workforce in order to manufacture the new product, the human resources department will have to hire and interview more personnel.

Not all organizations run efficiently. Many of them are more prone to dysfunction. Barriers often develop between different functional areas, which can lead to endless problems. Territorial disputes arise over issues of authority, decision-making, and control. Business people refer to the barriers between different functional areas as *silos*. Picture a large storage silo on a farm that protects the grain from the outside environment. Higher level managers are responsible for limiting these silos to minimize damage to the organization's effectiveness. You'd think a CEO could just order her employees to cooperate—in companies however, as in life, it's not that simple.

A small organization may have one person oversee multiple functions. Such jobs are demanding, but they are a great way to gain a comprehensive view of a company's internal operations.

Large and small companies contract with outside firms for their assistance with a particular project. For example, a small firm may not employ a fulltime attorney to handle legal matters. When legal questions arise, they'll purchase legal services from a law firm. A university may have a large internal department of legal affairs, but it will hire outside counsel for complex or criminal matters. Many grad students are employed by firms in the consulting industry. Companies might hire a consulting firm to implement a new sales plan, or to prepare an environmental impact report on a proposed building site.

In some cases, companies actually eliminate an entire department. They will then contract with another company to perform these duties. Hiring people outside the firm to perform functional duties is referred to as *outsourcing*. All universities once hired their own janitors. Most janitorial services are currently outsourced to separate entities. Outsourcing is used to reduce the number and cost of fulltime employees.

The media has drawn a great deal of attention to the large number of manufacturing jobs that have been outsourced to Asia. Since wages are lower in these countries, it is more economical for U.S. corporations to outsource rather than to hire fulltime employees in the United States. Shifting jobs to another country is sometimes called "offshoring."

When you select a functional area, you are selecting an occupation or profession. In business, the use of the word *profession* has been expanded beyond individuals with advanced education and experience (e.g., physicians, attorneys, accountants, etc.). Business people refer to themselves as marketing professionals, human resource professionals, and sales professionals. There are associations affiliated with these professionals that provide member services such as education, employment, public relations, and lobbying. These associations provide a wealth of informative materials you can use to research different occupations.

When you choose a type of work, you should consider the same factors you used when selecting an industry. In most cases your skills and knowledge will be the determining variables. Researchers will feel more at home in a research department, and education and training will be appealing to teachers. If you have good people skills, you might work in human resources, marketing, or sales.

Learning Curve

It will take time to understand the details of different industries and functional areas. While there are many subtleties to learn, you can gather enough information to narrow your job search. The best way to learn is by talking with people in the various industries and occupational areas. You can strike up these conversations in everyday situations. People love to talk about their jobs. Once you get them started talking about themselves, it may be difficult to wrap up the discussion.

A more formal approach to these conversations is commonly called an "informational interview." You may already know someone you'd like to talk with for 30–60 minutes. Contact them and arrange a time to speak by phone or in person. The purpose of setting up an informational interview is to develop a detailed understanding of the person's work. You'll be able to ask questions about their occupational area and their professional organization. Chapter 21 provides a detailed guide to arranging and conducting informational interviews.

Although you have several important decisions ahead of you, don't think of it as a burden. Picture yourself in a clothing store or bakery. You're selecting among so many positive alternatives, you can't help but make the right choice.

9

Many Paths to Your Goal

The path to a business job is very different from the route to becoming a professor. The academic process is linear. The challenging part is completing graduate school and showing evidence of productive scholarship. Then, as you are finishing your Ph.D., you'll begin to scan job postings and announcements from schools with available slots. You send your vitae and hope someone on the selection committee will be interested in your research interests and skill sets. Next are the interviews and job talks, until at last you receive an offer.

The hiring process in academics is relatively straightforward and direct (i.e., job announcements, submit CV, interview, selection, hiring). You've already selected your industry (education) and sub-sector (higher education) and your type of work (professor). Because you want to be a professor in a specific discipline, you need only apply at colleges and universities that have openings in your department.

Your career path in business will be more convoluted. Since you aren't certain of the kind of job you want, you may have to explore several different industries. A willingness to work in many different functional areas will necessitate an even broader search. You won't receive responses when you submit most resumes, and it's almost impossible to talk to a hiring manager directly. The route to a job in business looks more like a bowl of spaghetti than a single, straight line. Unlike Oz and academics, there is no yellow brick road to your first business job. Instead, there are many paths, with many twists and turns. Here are some of the complexities you'll learn to negotiate.

Highly desirable jobs are not widely advertised, so you may never learn about them. The people who are hired for the majority of these jobs hear about them through word-of-mouth. By the time you hear about them, they're often already filled, and not by a job seeker like yourself. Most companies have a policy of hiring from within. Laws require companies to publicly announce openings, but many jobs are first announced to current employees. While companies will advertise the position and review all the submitted resumes, they may have already vetted a highly qualified internal candidate. Internal candidates have another advantage. Some of the job qualifications may require an intimate knowledge of the company's internal processes. As a result, only a truly exceptional outsider would have a chance of being hired.

In other cases, an executive may want to hire a new assistant. It's very early in the hiring process and there may be no official job description, budget line, or announcement. It's only when the company hears of an excellent candidate that they take any action to fill the slot. To get the job, you need to have someone in your network who can tell the executive about your outstanding abilities.

You need to be on several simultaneous paths to get your first job. It's not going to be as simple as developing a resume, sending it off to an email address, and waiting for the interview invitations to arrive. A relatively passive approach is unlikely to produce the job you want. You'll need to adopt a more active stance.

Business is Personal

"Its business, it's not personal" is one of the lines made famous by the classic film *The Godfather*. While organized crime might not be personal, business is personal—*very* personal. Gatekeepers are involved in every stage of the hiring process, including the final decision to hire *you*. If you can make one of these gatekeepers aware of your talents, your odds will go up dramatically.

When it comes to your first job, someone will probably tell you about the opening, and a friend of a friend will get your resume to the right individual. A similar process sometimes occurs in academia. If your major professor has a personal relationship with someone at a school that's hiring, you may learn about the opening before anyone else. Your CV could receive special consideration and your professor's friend could become an advocate inside the hiring committee.

In business, you must create your own network of personal connections. Since you are starting from scratch, your network of social friends and relatives will serve as the foundation for your business network. The size and quality of this business network will be a critical determinant of the speed with which you find a job. Later chapters will provide detailed guidance on how to build and expand your business network. Let's jump ahead temporarily and examine how you'll use your business network.

When reduced to essential elements, the job search is about selling. You're selling yourself to potential employers. You'll need to sell them on why you're a better choice for the position than your competition. Selling is often described as a numbers game. Imagine an old-time salesperson walking down the street making cold calls by knocking on doors. The more doors the salesperson knocks on, the more likely he'll make a sale. While there are many ways to increase your chance of making a successful sale, the fundamental wisdom remains true. The more doors you figuratively knock on (i.e., the more people you talk to), the closer you'll move to getting your job.

Metaphorically, a person in your network is behind each door. When you are in dire need of work, you hope the very first person will hire you. For better or worse, that dream is almost always a dream. A more realistic expectation is that when someone opens their door, they'll give you access to another door, and so on, until you reach your goal. Each step gets you closer, but there are no guarantees. It's a numbers game. Simply stated, the more people you contact, the better your chances of success.

The quality of your connections is as important as the number of your connections. One factor that will affect the quality of your network is the nature of your bond with each person. Family and friends will be among the first members of your network. These people are very valuable, because they know you and like you. They'll be willing to go out of their way to help you. They'll keep telling people about you and asking about possible job openings. And, they'll be encouraging and optimistic.

The usefulness of your network will also be dependent on the quality of your members' networks. Some individuals will have many connections (so-called super-connectors) and others will have very few. The more connections a person has, the more valuable he or she becomes. Interestingly, people in middle management often have the largest number of names in their Rolodex. On the other hand, people in high-level jobs are usually more influential with regard to hiring. A connection to a senior executive could open some very important doors. Once you select an industry and a type of work, individuals in these fields will have a greater potential to help you.

Timing adds another dimension of complexity to the process. The first time you talk to someone, they may be too busy to help you. Don't scratch them off your list. Things change rapidly in hiring, and it's important to check in regularly with the people in your network. Someone you spoke with three weeks ago may suddenly learn about an opening. If you aren't in regular communication, you might be overlooked. Matters of timing and how actively you maintain your network can be as important as the number and quality of your connections.

Sometimes, timing can be a matter of minutes, not days or weeks. Imagine you are at a meeting of your local alumni. You begin talking with Chris, an old classmate. After some small talk, you ask Chris if she knows anyone who is looking for a bright, hardworking person without much work experience. She doesn't know of anyone, but says she'll call you if anything changes. Thirty minutes later a stranger walks up and announces, "I'm Brian, and Chris told me I should talk with you about a job opening." Your initial conversation with Chris didn't seem very productive. In less than an hour, however, she connected you with Brian who could become your next boss.

Repetition works in advertising, and that's why we see the same ads again and again. You can put repetition to work for you by finding creative ways to regularly contact people in your network. You'll want your requests to match your degree of connection to each person. You can be much more forward with a close friend than with someone in your extended network. Be sure to express your gratitude for any assistance, even if it is only a phone call. Let them know you hope to repay their favor. After you are launched in your business career, remember how much you needed the help of virtual strangers. Be willing to extend yourself to others who are struggling to start their careers.

Your network can expand exponentially in size and quality. Each new person has the potential to connect you with someone in their network. The people in this more extended network won't know you very well, so your connection will be weak. A weak connection can be very useful if you're just seeking information. While a network is a string of ifs, maybes, possibilities, and probabilities, this is how you will eventually get a job.

You might send an email to someone you only know via your extended network: "Can you suggest anyone in the technology sector I could call for a short informational interview?" It doesn't take much effort to give you a name. If they trust you'll be respectful in communicating with the individual, they may also give you the necessary contact information, and give you permission to mention their name. For example, they may give you the name and phone number of one of their former roommates who is now a manager at Google. Because you're a friend of a friend, this individual is more likely to give you tips about breaking into the industry. And, if he hears of an upcoming opening, whose name will come to mind?

This kind of networking and follow-up is very common in business. Because it is less common in academia, grad students are sometimes hesitant to initiate these types of interactions. In the larger working world, networking is synonymous with business. Everyone uses this process. You will quickly discover that people are not only comfortable with these inquires, they're generally happy to help. As a result of helping you, the connection will be stronger, and you'll be willing to help when they contact you for assistance.

Of course, there are always a few people who will abuse these relationships. They'll be too pushy and make major demands on virtual strangers. An underlying rule of reciprocity operates in these exchanges. Business people assume you'll know when to stop your inquiries if they say, "Sorry, I don't really know anyone in the industry. How do you think the Yankees will do this year?"

One person in your network leads to another, who leads to another. It becomes a probability chain, and your chances of success increase as you add new links. One of these extended connections could be just the one you need. This person is hiring, or they have a friend inside another company that is looking for a bright person who's willing to learn.

The person in your network who hooked you up is not only helping you, he's also helping his friend. Therefore, he's more likely to get future assistance. Networking works to everyone's advantage and that's why it's so essential.

Several adages apply perfectly to the hiring process: "It's not what you know, it's who you know" . . . "You have to be in the right place at the right time" . . . "Timing is everything." These may sound like worn-out clichés, but they contain important truths that still hold today.

You may be ideally qualified, but if you don't have a connection inside the company, you won't get the job. You may be very talented, but there are other qualified people who could also do the job. Your network will help you stand out and give you an edge over your competition.

Being at the right place at the right time seems to imply you have to be sitting in the reception area when the boss decides to hire someone. You don't have to spend your days seated on an uncomfortable sofa in a stuffy waiting room reading old magazines. One of your contacts will be at a meeting in which the job is announced, and they'll call you.

This paean to networking doesn't mean you should ignore job websites and job listings in print publications. There are many possible paths to your goal and it will pay to try them all. Submit your resume to legitimate job postings that seem tailored to your qualifications and interests. Many people may respond to this one ad. so the competition can be fierce. If, however, you have the unique skills that match the job description you could be called for an interview and ultimately become the person they hire.

Although you should continue to respond to legitimate ads, remember you're much more likely to get a job through someone you know. Put the majority of your efforts into networking.

Search and Assist

You can turbo charge your network by forming a "Search and Assist" team. The idea is simple. A small group of people (4–6 works best) meets regularly to assist one another with the search for jobs. The members can be acquaintances or strangers, so long as they are united in the goal of assisting one another find a job. It's not a good idea to include people who all have similar credentials and are looking for exactly the same type of position.

The Search and Assist (S&A) members can help one another in many ways. At one meeting you might review resumes. At another, you might discuss ways to expand and utilize your business networks. S&A members can alert one another to jobs, and to websites with useful information and job listings. You can also role-play an interview situation and provide constructive feedback to improve one another's performance. S&A members can also recommend what you should wear to an interview. You might borrow a necktie or a string of pearls.

Most important, this committed band of fellow-travelers can sincerely praise and recognize the significance of each member's small steps toward a job. This personal support will be very important in Stage 3 of the change process.

You'll need to follow many paths to achieve your goal. Unlike the grad students who are looking for one job (professor), you'll need input from people from all kinds of fields in your invaluable network. Using your net, you'll land a job and begin your brilliant career.

10

What Do You Want To B?

After you've decided what you *don't* want—to pursue an academic career—you must tackle the other big question: what you *want*. This can be a daunting decision. It might feel as if this monumental choice will seal your fate for the rest of your working life. Plus, you have to make this selection with only a limited understanding of the job market. How do you decide *how to decide*?

The advice of many career counselors brings to mind Robert Frost's poem about the proverbial fork in the road. You can choose the most commonly recommended route, or the other one. Although it's not often recommended, the road less traveled could, as the poem says, make all the difference.

Do What Feels Right

What is the best way to choose a career? Many experts suggest you listen to your heart, do what you love, and follow your bliss. At times, however, the logic can appear almost ridiculously simplistic: If you like to walk on the beach, consider oceanography. Or, if you enjoy flowers, perhaps you should become a florist. This counsel to follow your heart works fine for people with a lifelong passion.

Unfortunately, many young adults are uncertain which path aligns with their heartfelt interest. They can't identify an inner voice, and when they do hear something, it's more often the sound of a choir rather than that of a soloist.

One proposed solution is to utilize psychological tests to reveal your personality traits, personal strengths, and deeper interests. There are many web sites and career counselors who will administer these tests and interpret the results. Some people find these tests useful as a starting point. While the results of personality tests are interesting, many people feel they already know themselves. For example, they're more of an introvert than extrovert; they lean toward being analytic rather than intuitive; they prefer structured over ambiguous situations; they're a leader more than a follower.

Some people express doubts about using a test to select their life's work. These tests are based on normative data. It represents a compilation of the interests of people in different occupations. Test-takers are then categorized according to the interests and values they express on the exams. It's assumed that if other people with interests similar to your own found satisfaction in a career, then you will too. In some ways career testing resembles online dating. You are matched with people with whom you share similarities. Since you both like reading, candlelight dinners, and Italian food, you should therefore like one another.

A Career with Learning Potential

Studies have tracked the average number of career changes a person makes during his or her working life. Notice that this isn't a simple measure of how often people change jobs. People frequently move from one company to another, but they continue to do the same kind of work. "Career change" means switching from one occupation to another. A teacher leaves the classroom and becomes a human resource specialist for the school district. While she is still in the same industry, she switched job functions and is now on a different career track. After ten years of corporate law, an attorney goes into commercial real estate. His career change takes him away from the law, although he still uses his legal training when writing contracts.

The mean number of career changes in a person's life varies from study to study but it is always above 1.0 and sometimes as high as 3.0. In the contemporary employment environment, virtually everyone makes one major career change during their lifetime, and many people make several before locating *the* job. You might validate this finding as you talk to people. For example, it's very common for people to switch into management.

Why do people switch careers with such frequency, especially after selecting a field they thought they would love? There are many reasons. They may have been young, naïve, or ill advised about the kind of work that would best suit their temperament. Somewhere along the road, they realized they'd be much happier doing something else. When discussing why it took so long to make a switch, people invariably volunteer that they wish they'd made the change sooner.

Many people slowly evolve into a new career by creating a job inside their current company. Imagine an accountant who realizes she finds more pleasure dealing with clients than conducting audits or preparing tax reports. Since many of her associates are more comfortable with numbers, they ask her for assistance when talking with their clients. She develops a passion for putting people at ease and helping them understand the complexity of their financial reports. In time, she fills a newly created position as the firm's client relations specialist. She is the interface between the accounting firm and the people they serve.

While some people may be able to predict which career track will bring them happiness, most of us only figure out what we really want to do by doing something we *don't* like. Initially the job sounds great, but after a year or two, you realize it's not for you. It's an ironic truth: you'll probably discover your true occupational calling by doing work you don't really enjoy. This is because we learn by *doing* not just by thinking. Your first job will get you involved with the business world, and you'll discover the things you do well and the things that aren't your forte. You'll also begin to appreciate the intricacies of business and discover the wide range of alternative jobs that might be better suited to your personality.

From this perspective, the ideal first job is one that not only provides learning opportunities, but serves as a springboard to your next job. Too often people pick a job based on how much money they'll earn, or because of an organization's prestige. In the long run these factors are important. While you're still discovering what you want to do, it makes more sense to choose a job that offers the best context for learning and growing.

What Do You Have to Learn?

Unlike Tolstoy's happy families who are all alike, businesses become successful in many different ways. You'll want to learn why one company succeeded with a particular business strategy and why another went into a nosedive. If you like big-picture thinking, you'll be fascinated to learn how corporations make their major strategic choices. For example, after building gas-guzzling cars for decades, General Motors is finally shifting its strategy to build more fuel-efficient vehicles. Alternatively, if you appreciate the interconnections inside systems, business will give you a new appreciation of what it takes to profitably bring a product to market.

If you are intrigued by interpersonal dynamics, you can study both the conflicts and harmonies that exist inside every company. It's common to find disagreements between the departments of finance, marketing, production, distribution, and sales. Make it a point to develop relationships with people in other departments and functional areas within your organization. In addition to learning your own job, you'll learn how your job is connected to the other parts of your firm.

You'll also want to learn more about your industry. What are the attributes of a successful firm versus one that is in trouble? Is your company on a track for improved performance? The history of industries and their leaders is a fascinating study. Government rules, regulations, and tax policies play an increasingly important role in all industries. You may want to develop a better understanding of the latter factors, especially if you're working in a highly regulated industry such as insurance or transportation.

Then there are the politics. Office politics aren't unique to business. You had to quickly grasp the politics of your grad program and your professors. In analyzing the politics of your company, begin by identifying the key players. How did they get to the top? Did they begin in a specific department? Have they followed a similar path? How did they build alliances with more senior people in the organization? What personal attributes do they possess? Who challenges their decisions? How do these up-and-coming people express their opposition? Watch the interplay of cooperation and competition among the different groups who are supposedly all working for a common purpose. Business people enjoy speculating about organizational politics, so you will find many willing teachers.

As you observe people ascending the fast track of advancement, try to determine how they got there, and why others remain stuck in the same job. You may not want to emulate all the actions of these single-minded achievers, but you can learn ways to advance your career. It's also important to identify how and why people sabotage their career opportunities.

You should also investigate the training courses your company provides. If you have access to this free education, learn as much as you can. Get to know the people who work in the training department. Perhaps you'll want to explore this area as a career.

In addition to meeting people inside your current company and industry, set goals to establish relationships with people in other industries. They'll add to your overall understanding of the business, and they'll keep you informed about job opportunities outside your present sphere. Business people love to talk about the job market. They're always on the lookout for an outstanding prospect to bring into their organization. They're also interested in possible jobs for their next career move. When someone initially feels them out about a job at another company, they may say they're perfectly happy in their present job—but then quickly add, "Of course, there's no harm in looking."

Before you decide to move to another company, remain alert to openings within your own organization. Identify the departments that are growing and those that have reached a plateau. Try to learn about the internal promotion process. What does it take to become an outstanding internal candidate? Who should you know, and how can you learn about new openings? Who are the managers of the departments that interest you?

Before going public with your desire to move to another department, ascertain whether your boss demands absolute loyalty. If so, you'll want to keep your study of the internal advancement process to yourself. If you are fortunate to have a manager who encourages the growth and development of their direct reports, they might be willing to discuss your next career move.

In addition to learning about everything around you, devote some time to studying yourself. Become an observer of you. Recognize the situations in which you perform best. Which of your abilities enable you to stand out? What personal qualities do you need to develop or suppress? What parts of the job do you enjoy and which do you find boring? Which aspects of your industry engage you? Notice the kinds of people you seek out and those you avoid. If you're eating lunch every day with a group of people who criticize the company, find another table. The dark cloud hanging over these folks will quickly taint you in the eyes of anyone evaluating your potential.

Monitor your reaction to each new experience. Reread Chapter 2 on the J-Curve of Change, and follow your reactions during the different stages of your own personal metamorphosis. Analyze the factors that impact your moods. How do your ideas about working in the business world change from day to day? Watch the reactions of other new hires, and observe the behavior of people undergoing a major change, such as a promotion or demotion. Continually ask what lessons you learned today, and how these insights could help you improve.

The art of communication is complex, with many subtleties. Begin with the jargon. Business has endless acronyms and phrases (a glossary of business term is at JobsA2B.com). When you first start using this terminology, it may feel as though you're speaking a foreign language. You'll hear these words so frequently; they'll quickly become second nature. Don't refrain from using business jargon with your colleagues. It's a language they understand and it marks you as an "insider." It's called "talking the talk" in business. And, don't hesitate to use the word "we." You're part of the group, so use the pronoun that says "team."

At the same time you're learning about business, study your job and learn how to do it better. An outstanding record of performance will launch you to your next position. Schedule a meeting with your supervisor and discuss her specific expectations. The two of you may be able to work together to establish quarterly goals and quantitative metrics to measure your progress. In subsequent months, meet with her again for feedback and recommendations on how to improve. Listen carefully and confirm your understanding of her comments.

Some bosses say one thing but mean something else. Your co-workers will offer insights about how to read between the lines of your boss' public statements. Your success inside the company will depend on meeting your boss' expectations. Don't fall into the trap of doing what you think, or what someone else tells you. Does this sound similar to working with your major professor?

How much you learn in business is the same as in grad school—it's entirely up to you. By learning what's possible in business, you'll develop a deeper understanding of what's possible for you.

II

Get Activated

Anger, anxiety, failure, discouragement, fear, and panic do not make the process of changing careers sound appealing. These are the common emotions associated with Stages 2 and 3 of the change process. When these feelings begin to build, most people consider giving up or escaping. While tempting, these are not productive ways to deal with the situation. The *activation* techniques described below provide a constructive path of action, even when you're not feeling motivated.

Head or Feet First?

The popular advice to people who are feeling discouraged is to "think positive." Good thoughts and a positive attitude will supposedly enable you to achieve anything you want. Care to walk on burning coals? Wonderful as it is to feel good about yourself, and to have high self-esteem, just thinking good thoughts isn't enough. You must also take action. When thoughts alone aren't getting the result you want, try activation.

Activation is a toolkit of practical techniques you can employ when you get discouraged. As the name implies, instead of focusing on the thoughts in your head, activation emphasizes the actions you take with your feet. It stresses the small things you can do to escape your lethargy and break through your procrastination.

By taking not just small, but tiny steps, you'll begin to experience little victories. Building a history of small successes creates a solid foundation for your self-esteem. Rather than just having happy thoughts, your self-confidence will be grounded in your own real-world experience.

Getting Down to Ground Level

We've heard the wisdom that you begin a change by taking "baby steps." What exactly are baby steps, and how do you create them? When most people try to break a goal down into sub-steps, they use words that are up at a very *high altitude*. The altitude metaphor refers to words that are generalizations or conceptually abstract. Included here are allusions to internal psychological states: get motivated, apply yourself, be enthusiastic, adopt a different perspective, and (a favorite in business) think outside the box.

Too often when people attempt to translate baby steps into actions, they figuratively grab the Thesaurus and substitute a new high-altitude synonym for the original word. As a result, we get stuck in a holding pattern. ("Replace that negative attitude with a positive one. Be optimistic. Show enthusiasm. The glass is half full as well as half empty.") Ground level words describe concrete behaviors. The difference between high-altitude and ground level words can be illustrated with a crucial job search task: Build a business network.

To build a business network, you could take these sub-steps:

1.   Expand the number of people in your network.
2.   Get to know more people.
3.   Be assertive when you talk to new people.

While these suggestions seem like a reasonable starting point, they don't specify exactly what you should do. Here are some ways to reinterpret these statements.

You could *expand* the number if you:
    Think about more people.
    Imagine people you'd like to have in your network.
You could *get to know* more people by:
    Being friendly with people.
    Striking up conversations with strangers.
    Getting out in public more often.
    Making new friends.
Being *assertive* suggests you should:
    Be more confident.
    Feel good about yourself.
    Express your own opinions.

Do any of these statements tell you exactly what to do? They're a little more specific, but it's still unclear how you are supposed to act. While each may spark a few new thoughts, they're unlikely to produce much action. That's because the verbs are still up at a very high altitude. They need to be translated down to specific, ground level behavior.

The translation process is built around one simple question: What action should I take? The emphasis is on *action*, not thoughts, feelings or generalizations. Break the high-level verb into things you can actually do. There are many ways to bring new people into your network. Consider this ground level example: "You'll need to set aside some time. Choose a room without distractions. You'll need a method to record the names."

These all sound viable, but what else should you do? You could *think* of people you've known in different contexts or situations. Here's how these ideas might be stated as an action plan for the week.

> Pick three days between Monday and Friday to work on your list for a total of 30 minutes. Break the time into three 10-minute segments and spread them out over three days. Make the list immediately after your evening meal. On day one, take 10 minutes to list your close friends and anyone you know from grad school. You can work on your computer or use a paper and pen. On the second day, take 10 minutes and make a list of your relatives. Include extended family members who you know more by name than by actual contact. On the third day, compile the names of people from undergrad school, friends you grew up with, and people you worked with on any jobs.

Does this information offer a more precise plan of how to proceed? Does it seem like an easier way to get started taking action? Instead of turning into a major project, you only need 10 minutes. If that's too much, how about 5 minutes? In truth, once people start taking action they often work longer than they planned.

The word *think* refers to something you ruminate in your mind. "Thinking" can be transformed into action by giving structure to what you think about each day. In this illustration, the time and date are specific, as well as the action you'll take to record the names that come to mind. Clearly, there are many ways to translate a sub-step into a ground level action. This is only one example.

You can practice your skill at making ground level descriptions by selecting some of the earlier sub-steps. For example, how would you go about *imagining* the people you'd like to add to your network? Would you like them to work at certain companies? What skills and experiences would you like these people to have? What kind of work would they be doing? Is there anyone on campus you'd like to meet and possibly include on your list?

Use the following phrases to practice your skill at getting down to ground level.

Be friendly with people.
Get out in public more often.
Be more confident.

Expanding upon a specific situation can also help bring ground level into focus. If you were *friendlier*, what would you say to someone seated next to you on a bus, train, or plane? If you can't think of any specific behaviors, imagine a person who is very friendly (or, confident, determined, etc.). What would a very friendly person say in this situation? Breaking the action into a sequence of behaviors can also help. What is the first thing I would do; what would be the second, the third...? These action questions will help you get down to ground level language.

An old aphorism suggests that god is in the details. The details are what is important. They are the fundamental reality. Small, constructive actions will move you toward your goal.

When you talk in ground level language, you outline a precise recipe to follow. If ground level action still feels like a lot of work, then take it down even lower. Ten minutes can be reduced to five. If meeting ten strangers and delivering your elevator pitch is too much, break it down. Just say hello to ten strangers with a smile on your face. Are ten strangers too many? How about five?

Minimize Obstacles

When you don't feel like acting, how large an obstacle does it take to convince yourself to put on the brakes? Even the smallest barrier can act as a deterrent. Return to the example about taking ten minutes to make a list of names for your network. Imagine these thoughts: "I have too many distractions here at home to concentrate on making a list. How can I make a list when I don't have a clean tablet and my desk is a mess?" Remove these tiny barriers, and thereby minimize the rationalizations you use to avoid taking action.

Select a 10-minute window when you're home alone. Put your cell phone in another room. Turn off the television, and your iPod. You might convince yourself to postpone the task because your printer is out of ink. Rather than putting it off for another day, make the list on your computer. Buy an ink cartridge tomorrow and then print the list.

When small things start to interfere, find ways to work around them. If you were in a dire emergency, you'd find a way to negotiate the barriers.

Get Assistance

Friends and family can help you begin a new task or push past a problem. Don't hesitate to ask for assistance or problem-solving advice. How do your friends deal with procrastination? What gets them moving? If the answers are up at a high level, practice getting them down to ground level with your questions You could teach friends to ask these action questions. Their questions will stimulate you to think of new ground level answers.

Your Search and Assist group is an ideal place to get encouragement and advice. Since your group is familiar with the job search process, their answers may already be down at ground level.

Front-Loading Rewards

The first step over the cliff from Stage 1 to Stage 2 of the J-Curve of Change can be frightening. You know you're going to make some missteps. Many grad students have a history of outstanding performance and are personally uncomfortable with mistakes. At the beginning of any new venture, you're bound to make errors, do foolish things, and wander up a few blind alleys. When you repeatedly strike out, it's easy to become discouraged.

Words of encouragement and praise can be very motivating. Let your friends and S&A group know how much you need their positive feedback. You may want to bring your request down to ground level: "I'd like some praise for bravely making a cold call to a stranger." People who care about you want to praise you. Your request will give them permission to express their admiration.

Mistakes are inevitable. Use mistakes as learning experiences, and tell your friends how you're going to improve in the future. Your friends will praise you for your persistence and acknowledge your efforts to push forward

Small goals create opportunities to congratulate yourself. For example, you deserve to be proud that you compiled a network list in 30 minutes. The list didn't exist Monday, but by Friday evening, there it is! What's your next small step?

Handling Negative Emotions

How can you most effectively deal with the inevitable setbacks? Your self confidence may get a bit shaky, especially when you're knocked down several times in the same week. Go ahead, acknowledge your frustration and disappointment, but set some time limits. By endlessly recycling the event, you'll only prolong your discomfort. How can you get refocused on action?

Take your mind out of the doldrums and resist nonproductive emotions. We all develop personal solutions for coping with negative feelings. Video games, television, the Internet, or spending time with friends can get your mind off your malaise. Physical activity is a great way to cleanse unwanted thoughts and feelings. Get outside and take a walk. A change of scenery can work wonders.

The sooner you get back on task the better. Even the smallest steps can help neutralize any remaining negative feelings. Ultimately, you must get back to ground level. Try and visualize a stalk of bamboo in a wind storm. When the wind hits the bamboo, it tries to resist but is eventually pushed backward. The bamboo bends and then snaps back into place. You can bend by acknowledging your frustration. Once you've given voice to these feelings, snap back with ground level steps.

Keep this activation toolkit handy, especially when your motivation and self-confidence are lagging. The cumulative effect of your ground level actions (both the successful actions and the ones you learned from) will change how you think and feel about yourself. Your small successes will bolster your self-confidence and embolden you to take on still greater challenges.

12

Pre-Occupations

You don't have to do everything at once. You can begin your journey into the business world by degrees. Plus, you can learn about business without interfering with your regular graduate school studies. Professors and colleagues in your program don't have to know about this new dimension of your life unless you volunteer the information. These "pre-occupational" activities can vary from minutes to hours a week depending on your schedule. The following list is arranged in order from the least to the most demanding on your schedule.

30 Minutes a Week

Journal articles and scholarly books fill much of your time each day. Could you find 30 minutes a week to scan the *Wall Street Journal* (WSJ)? You can locate it in your university and local public library. Your university may give you access to the WSJ online edition. You can read it daily in the library, or go through all six issues on the weekend.

For grad students, WSJ will take you on a informative adventure and into a different world. Regardless of your familiarity with business, you'll learn a great deal from this publication. Read the headlines and scan the sections. Even business people don't read the WSJ cover to cover. People skim it for stories that pertain to their current situation. Understanding the format of the paper will enable you to know where to look.

The WSJ has four sections. The first section covers topics that are of interest to a general business audience. Begin by scanning columns one and two on the front page. They give a useful executive summary of the day's important events. Because it's a business newspaper, most of the stories focus on business and finance. The editorial bias is clearly pro-business and may be surprising to people of a different political orientation. There are daily book reviews that will be easily accessible and informative to any graduate student.

Section 2 of the paper is called *Marketplace* and many of the stories describe the current strategy, ad campaigns, marketing and sales results (e.g., Monday has box office numbers for the prior week) for various corporations. You may be interested in a story about the companies and products you use (e.g., Google, Starbucks, Wal-Mart, and smart phones). *Money and Investing* is the title of Section 3, and it's filled with numbers. Unless you are investing in stocks, you will probably skip these pages. You don't have to delve into the stock market just to get a job in business.

You're sure to find something of interest in Section 4, *Personal Journal.* The content focuses on topics that impact the personal lives of adults. There's also a very practical column on personal technologies. The Friday and Saturday weekend editions are more relaxed, with great film reviews, a fascinating wine column, and photos of the mansion you'll call home in a few years. Using only four minutes to scan each of the six WSJ papers per week, you'll still have time to also check out one or two business magazines.

Fortune and *Business Week* have longer business stories, but also contain brief news summaries. *Business Week* has a column on current trends in personal technology. You can survey the contents in a few minutes. Other business magazines focus on more specific topics. *INC.* emphasizes small businesses, and *Fast Company* stresses the technology sector. There are a plethora of magazines and trade journals that cover specific industries. Most of these publications also have informative websites.

As your area of interest becomes more focused, you can concentrate on a few industries (e.g., insurance and healthcare) or companies (e.g., Traveler's, Blue Cross, Kaiser Permanente) and their publications. You might also scan *The Economist,* which has a more global focus, plus a sophisticated section on the arts and sciences. *The Harvard Business Review* has somewhat more technical articles about business management.

If you can invest another 15 minutes per week, you could glance at the business sections in two other outlets. The business section of the *New York Times* (NYT) is more accessible than the WSJ. The Sunday edition of the NYT has a "Careers" column that addresses the job search and related job issues. You can find stories about companies in your vicinity by scanning the business section of your local paper.

Do you listen to your car radio or iPod during your commute, or while you're at the gym? Tune into the daily broadcast of "Marketplace" on National Public Radio. The program covers topics of general business interest and expends only a few minutes on the daily stock results. The host's upbeat tone will speed your time in traffic and improve your workout.

One Hour a Week

Universities offer free or low-cost software courses. Take advantage of this opportunity to develop your quantitative skills. Gain at least a basic familiarity with QuickBooks and Excel, as well as with other programs in Microsoft Office. Without becoming a specialist, learn the basics of graphics programs and web design. A three-hour course will make you a more attractive job candidate. You may also qualify for free or low-fee courses offered by community colleges, high schools, or local libraries.

Courses on the job search process may also be available from different organizations in your local community. Some religious organizations provide workshops for people entering the job market. You'll learn more details in Chapter 20, but your university's career center will offer many free seminars and workshops on all elements of the job search process. If you invest ten hours each semester to acquire new software skills or career information, you'll grow as a person and improve your job opportunities.

Two Hours a Week

Expanding your social network is critical. The discussion in Chapter 11 of ground level language gives you a clear roadmap for how to begin. When you speak with members of your network, remember to end every discussion by. asking if they can connect you with any of their associates or contacts. Get names and numbers. Better yet, ask if they'd alert each person by email or phone that you'll be contacting them.

At parties or casual get-togethers, make it a point to talk with people about their jobs. Ask for their business card if you think you might look them up in the future. Check the calendar of your university's Business School for events and speeches. You'll be able to talk with the other attendees before and after the lecture.

Don't be worried about what you'll say to these strangers. People love to talk about their jobs, so you'll have an easy point of departure. You'll need to be ready with your elevator pitch (Chapter 15) when they turn their questions on you.

Check the schedule of local bookstores for presentations by authors. Pay particular attention to books on business and economics. The audience will be composed of people you might want to meet. Plus, these presentations offer a convenient way to keep up with the latest business ideas.

As you meet people and learn about their work, decide whether to include them in your business network. You might one day contact these individuals for information about your job search. Not every new acquaintance will be appropriate for your network. Set a personal goal to add one or two people per week to your network. By semester's end, you'll be impressed at the number of new and interesting people you've met.

Three Hours a Week

Your goal is to interview one business person per week. These conversations will increase your knowledge about jobs, industries and organizations. Whether conducted in person or on the phone, each interview should only take about 30 minutes. Make sure you always follow up with an email or handwritten note.

The details of this type of "informational interview" are described in Chapter 21. You can list the names of people you'd like to interview. Your business network will be a useful asset. Begin by interviewing key people in your network. Ask for their recommendations of anyone who might be willing to offer their perspective on a particular company or industry.

Let's face it, these people are doing you a favor. Let them pick a convenient time and place. Make it clear up front that your only goal is to learn about their job and their company. Conclude these discussions by asking if you can contact them with any additional questions. If they agree, they have implicitly added themselves to your business network. Informational interviews are a well established part of business and the individual will be flattered that a bright young person wants to talk with them.

During your daily life on campus you can combine network expansion with informational interviews. Go to the areas where people commonly eat lunch, and look for individuals who appear to work at the university. If someone is alone at a table, ask if you can sit with them. Begin by asking if they work on campus. Explain that you are a grad student who is interested in learning more about the administrative aspects of the university. Ask how their department contributes to the university. What part of their job is most enjoyable? Queries about career history and future plans are sure to spark more discussion.

If you think you'll have additional questions later, ask if you might set up a time to talk at greater length.

You can strike up similar conversations when you visit any administrative office on campus (e.g., the graduate school, the registrar, financial aid, or the cashier's office). It's easy to talk with people who work on campus, plus you can add them to your business network. If you need a part-time job on campus, you now have someone to use as a referral.

Five Hours a Week

Volunteering with a nonprofit organization is an easy way to improve your knowledge of business. Helping other people is a great way to help yourself when you're feeling discouraged. Although these organizations measure their effectiveness in terms of the services they provide rather than in dollars earned, many aspects of their organization directly parallel for-profit companies.

When you volunteer, it is vitally important that you assist with the administrative and business activities. At the Humane Society, you might work in the office—perhaps recruiting and scheduling other volunteers. You could help organize a fundraising event, or write press releases, rather than taking care of the animals. You never know which of your talents an organization will find useful (e.g., technology, writing, or research skills) until you volunteer.

The ability to set a flexible work schedule is another advantage of volunteering. You can usually create a schedule that doesn't conflict with your grad school commitments. Many not-for-profits are busier at certain times of the year. If you're available during these time frames, the organization's leaders will be very appreciative. For example, they may have an annual spring fundraising event, or special activities at Christmas.

If your graduate studies allow any free time, you could take courses outside your discipline. Check the catalogue for classes in the business school that might prepare you for a particular career track. An undergraduate class on finance for non-finance majors would stand out during an interview, and could be an asset in numerous job situations. Talk to the professor during the registration period and explain your status before enrolling in classes outside your major.

Five-Plus Hours a Week

If your schedule permits even more time, you might consider an internship or a part-time job. Internships are basically volunteer programs in a company or nonprofit organization. Some companies rotate a new set of interns three times a year. Ideally, you'll have a supervisor who will meet with you to explain the operations and offer feedback about your performance. It has become common for adults returning to the workplace to use internships, or "returnships," to find their way into a job.

In addition to the free labor, businesses often use internships as an opportunity to get a close-up look at a future job candidate. Although companies will make it clear that there is no guarantee of fulltime employment, an intern will have a definite advantage in case a job opens up. Internships with particular companies (e.g., technology and consulting) and certain industries (e.g., entertainment and publishing) are highly competitive. You can learn about internships through your career center on campus. You need to apply early for most internships. You may also go through a lengthy screening and interview process.

Jobs on campus can be very convenient, so you might investigate these part-time jobs. Again, you want a job where you can work in the business and administrative areas of the university. In addition to learning about the business of higher education, you may also acquire skills that will better qualify you for a future job.

It is very common for both undergraduate and graduate students working part time on campus to eventually move into fulltime positions. These jobs are in the grey zone. They're basically business jobs, but they're located on campus. You're able to enjoy the intellectual atmosphere of a university while you earn money. If you enjoy working directly with students, the offices of Student Life, Housing, and International Students may be of interest. Working part time in the advisement services department of the university could lead to a permanent career.

Many administrative offices on campus have important links to the business community (e.g., the alumni association or the university's development office). Development (or advancement) is a common euphemism for the people who raise money. Alumni are a prime source of contributions. By working in this department you'll acquire many skills that could easily transfer to jobs outside the university. You'll also come in contact with many individuals in the business world.

You can become an entrepreneur by starting your own tutoring, editing or consulting practice. Undergraduates and graduate students may seek your expertise or statistical skills for their classes or research projects. Many students also need "editorial" assistance on papers or a thesis. Editing jobs can be classified from *light* to what is euphemistically called *heavy*. Light refers to the common and important work of making minor stylistic and grammatical changes. In heavy editing you do most of the actual writing. Make sure you specify up front what you're willing to do, and how much you charge.

Starting your own business will allow you to create a flexible schedule. It's also a great way to become savvy about business. The fact that you had the entrepreneurial drive to start your own business will stand out on your resume. Occasionally (Michael Dell, who started Dell Computers in a dorm room, is a wonderful example), it's possible to establish a steady income while working as a consultant to other students.

Make volunteering, or working part time, a personal project, and commit to this important opportunity to learn about business. You may need to sacrifice some of your relaxation time, but you'll be making a substantial investment in your future.

Creating a Transition Toolkit

13

A Brand New You

What's your top-of-the-mind reaction to:

Starbucks vs. Dunkin' Donuts

Ford vs. Toyota

Apple vs. Microsoft PC?

The implicit beliefs and assumptions people have about a company and its products are referred to as its brand, or brand identity. Corporate identities vary along dimensions such as quality, status, reliability, creativity, price, and customer service. A company's identity is based in large part on their efforts to influence consumers' opinions. Businesses pay enormous sums to marketing professionals to create and promote their brand identity. Companies hope to influence the way customers think about their products. These beliefs can determine what and where people buy, especially when people are unfamiliar with the competing products.

Brands are created by companies (Tiffany or Wal-Mart), organizations (Republican or Democratic Party), universities (Harvard or Indiana University of Pennsylvania) and individuals (Obama or McCain). One day on campus, look at the different brand identities conveyed by each student. Notice how they use their clothing, hair, body art, and mannerisms to convey information about their personal identities.

Most corporations want their brand to be concise and easy to read, so they focus on only one, two, or three attributes. A brand uses shorthand—it says a lot with a few images, colors, and words. Brands highlight the positives and neglect to mention any negatives.

Apple Computer Corporation ran a series of ads featuring two actors. Both men were in their thirties, but one seemed older than the other. Dressed in a white shirt and tie, and a few pounds overweight, the one called "PC" resembled Bill Gates. The younger-looking actor dressed in a relaxed style. Mr. PC always seemed to be having one problem after another, while Mac, the one who resembled a young Steve Jobs, appeared more easygoing and immune to problems.

Apple used the ads to both define its brand and to try to alter the brand image of its competitor. PC appeared bloated, fussy, and burdened with problems, while Mac was slim, stylish and worry-free. The important dimension of price would be a negative for Apple, so it was never mentioned. In response, Microsoft produced ads centered on creating happy customers by saving them money.

Have you ever thought about your brand identity? If you have a website or Facebook page, you are already creating an online identity. What traits do people associate with you? Are these the characteristics you want to put forward? Do you want to convey the same identity to professors and fellow students that you want to communicate to business people? You might want to emphasize certain personal characteristics for the academic world, while underscoring others for business.

Your brand identity will be of continuing importance when you search for a job. Although first impressions can be misleading, they can still make a lasting impact. The first impression you make will affect how people treat you. If you create a positive impression, people will want to know you, help you in your search, and hire you. Given the importance of your identity, you should carefully consider how you want to be perceived and remembered.

Determining Your Identity

How are you perceived right now? What is your identity? Pick five to ten words that best describe you. You might list:

intelligent	*scholarly*
thorough	*friendly*
responsible	*reliable*
thoughtful	*optimistic*
curious	*inquisitive*

Now reduce this list to five words by combining similar adjectives.

In a sense *reliable* seems to encompass *responsible*, as well as *thorough*. *Intelligent* and *thoughtful* overlap, with *intelligent* being the stronger word. *Optimistic* and *positive* are almost the same, and *curious* and *inquisitive* describe yet another dimension. *Friendly* stands by itself. The list is now refined to: *reliable; intelligent, friendly, optimistic* and *curious*.

After compiling your list, ask several friends to give their impression of your key attributes. To help them get started, ask them to jot down words that capture your *personality*, a few words that describe your *abilities*, and two or three words about your *interpersonal style* or manner. Encourage them to write down the first words that come to mind. Collect their comments and reduce their lists to five to ten key words.

Your friends may have described you in words that are more suitable to interpersonal relations than to business. If so, replace their words with synonyms that have a stronger business connotation. More specifically, you want to be identified with traits that will stand out to an interviewer. When hiring someone, organizations are primarily concerned with one fundamental question: What can this person do to help the company grow and become more efficient? Use words that suggest how you can help the company achieve its business goals. Employers also want someone who will fit in and not cause problems, so include at least one word that conveys this information.

Now combine your friends' lists with your own. Imagine the first column below is *your* list and the second column lists the qualities proposed by your friends. Once again, condense both lists down to five key words or phrases.

reliable	*warm*
intelligent	*analytic*
friendly	*helpful*
optimistic	*questioning*
curious	*enthusiastic*
	easygoing

Analytic sounds more businesslike than intelligent. *Reliable* is more encompassing than *responsible*. *Optimistic* and *enthusiastic* are similar, and while they are used in the business world, the word *positive* also conveys an attitude about life. *Questioning* might imply that you challenge everything, while *curious* makes you sound inquisitive. How about using *inventive* or *creative* to convey this aspect of your nature? *Warm, easygoing,* and *helpful* make you sound like a great friend, but are these words strong enough for business? Businesses often use sports metaphors, so you might capture the tenor of these qualities with the phrase *team player*.

Based on this analysis, your brand represents someone with these five attributes:

Analytic
Reliable
Creative
Positive
Team player

These qualities will form the foundation of your brand. In this book they'll be referred to as your *strengths*. You'll use this list of strengths in many ways. They'll be at the core of your elevator pitch, and will make up the backbone of your resume.

The above exercise is hypothetical and is meant to illustrate how to gather and condense information about your strengths. When you conduct your own brand analysis, your traits may or may not be the same. For example, your brand might include words such as independent, leader, determined, and goal oriented. You could review your final list of strengths with a few members of your business network. Ask their advice on words that will best communicate your strengths and brand to business people.

Conveying Your Identity

The principles used by corporations to communicate their brands can be adapted to personal use. Branding professionals focus on at most three key elements of a company's identity, and so should you. It's difficult for people to remember more than three traits unless they're printed. Select the three strengths that you think will be most meaningful to a particular hiring director. When applying for a job in financial services (where trust and brain power are important), you might emphasize *reliable, analytic,* and *team player.* For a job in entertainment or marketing (where innovation and emotion are important) you might focus on *creative, positive* and *team player.*

Consistent repetition facilitates memory is another important branding principle. Companies try to embed their brand identity into every aspect of their products and marketing practices. What are the attributes of the Apple iPhone? It's innovative, has a great design, and is easy to use. Notice how these concepts could also describe Apple computers and iPods. In politics, repetition is referred to as "staying on message." National political parties try to have their leaders repeat the same message in speeches and in interviews.

"The Daily Show with Jon Stewart" frequently plays video clips of politicians repeating the same phrase over and over again. This redundancy looks contrived and humorous when edited together. In reality, however, you aren't as aware of the repetition, and it therefore becomes an effective way to convey a message.

Companies don't just stay on message in their advertisements; they incorporate it into the packaging of their products. It's also implicit in their logo. (Sometimes it's almost subliminal. Can you spot the arrow connoting movement and speed between the "E" and "x" in the FedEx logo?) From stationery to delivery trucks, organizations affix their logos to everything.

Have you ever studied the graphic design on your university's stationery? It's likely to appear on professors' and administrators' business cards as well. The logo was created by a design company as part of the university's effort to convey a consistent identity.

All major companies and universities get very particular about the use of their logo. Disney and McDonalds, among many others, can be litigious in protecting their branded images. There are people in the university who monitor how their logo is utilized. They are quick to correct anyone who strays from the prescribed guidelines. Employees refer to these enforcers as the "brand police." Their reprimands are as welcome as your mother telling you to comb your hair and change your shoes when you leave the house. She wants you to look a certain way because you represent your family's *brand*.

Just as companies are cognizant of both their products and how they are packaged, your personal brand identity is communicated in many ways. *What* you say, and *how* you say it, both broadcast your brand strengths. When you tell people you're looking for a job, you can expect the question: Why should a company hire you? Refining your brand and its strengths will prepare you to give a clear and concise answer.

Many job interviewers begin the meeting by asking you to describe your three most prominent attributes. While meant to be a simple question, the interviewer is listening to the things you identify as your strengths and how you communicate your answers. In later chapters, you'll learn to illustrate each strength with behavioral examples.

Academicians tend to think content is much more important than form, so they sometimes overlook appearances. In business, appearances matter—especially *first impressions*. In real estate, some houses have "curb appeal." Buyers like the looks of the property the moment they drive up and park. Products also try to use curb appeal to attract customers. Have you ever been influenced to buy a bottle of wine because of its well-designed label? Your manners and your clothing tell an important story about who you are. You want the message to be clear and consistent.

Can you picture the wardrobe of an analytic, reliable, team player? What about the dress of a creative, positive, team player? Do they wear the same style of clothing? Are their outfits in the same color tones? Are there differences in their accessories? What kind of glasses do they wear? How do they sit in a chair? What kind of writing instrument do they use? Can you picture their business cards?

You may disagree with the notion that "clothes make the man" (or woman), or that you should "dress for success," but when it comes to first impressions, these sayings carry useful wisdom. It's not surprising that Mr. PC in Apple's advertisements wears a coat and tie, while Mac is in a casual shirt and pants. It's not by chance that PC's coat is brown with a white shirt, and Mac wears muted blue tones.

The smallest of your actions can have a big impact on how people perceive you. Have you ever received a weak or limp handshake? What impression did it create? How do you feel toward someone whose voice is very loud? What about someone who speaks so softly you have to strain in order to hear them? The loud person is seen as insensitive, self-centered and inconsiderate. The quiet one seems to lack confidence and doesn't want to stand out.

What's in a name? Plenty. Your name is also part of your brand. It too sends a message. In general, diminutive names ending in an "e" sound (e.g., Jimmy, Debbie, Annie) are associated with childhood, while full names are linked to maturity and adulthood. This does not mean you must change your name to something formal, but you should be sure your name is consistent with your brand message. There is a reason so many film stars change their names (i.e., Archie Leach became Cary Grant).

If you are still having doubts about the importance of names, consider the role of titles. Just as Dick and Richard have slightly different connotations, the appellation "Dr." has a much greater impact than "Ms." and "Mr." One of the side benefits of earning a Ph.D. is that you can use the "doctor" prefix to your advantage in some situations.

The effect of any one of these elements may be small, but the cumulative effect could be significant. If they convey the same message, your brand identity will be reinforced. If these signals are out of alignment, people will receive mixed messages about who you are, and what you can do for their company. Someone with a clear, positive set of strengths is easier to remember and more likely to be hired. Work on defining and refining how you communicate your brand strengths.

An easy place to begin your branding process is to create a business card with your contact information. The card should have a simple design, and the information must be accurate. Your name, email address and phone number are sufficient. A job title below your name isn't necessary. Read every word and punctuation mark out loud, to proofread for errors.

Have you ever been handed a business card with someone's phone number crossed out and rewritten two or three times? How about a card that's bent, torn or even limp? It's very unprofessional. This type of card will reveal more about you than just your name and phone number.

Business cards can be inexpensively reproduced at a local office store. Print shops near campus are very experienced with business cards and will recommend paper (stick with white) and a type font. You'll need this card as you start building you business network. You're more likely to get a card if you have one to give.

14

Networking, Death, and Taxes

The word *network* began life as a noun. With the development of computer networks it morphed into a verb, and then finally transformed into a lifestyle with the rise of Facebook and Twitter. Social networks consume more attention than traditional television networks. Your social connections can serve as the foundation for the business network you'll create during your job search process. The people in your business network will be the most important determinant of how quickly you get a job.

Networking is an integral part of our social lives. You're networking when you ask a classmate questions about a class, assist a fellow student with her research, seek advice from a professor, and gossip with friends. Professors attend professional associations and scientific meetings—partially for the content, but also because they want to strengthen their network with professional colleagues.

Networking lubricates the machinery of business. It's so common that people have doubts about people who don't network. Some meetings are explicitly labeled as networking mixers. Office gatherings that appear primarily social (e.g., birthday and retirement parties, holiday get-togethers) always have an undercurrent of networking. Local meetings of college alumni are prime occasions for networking.

Networking is part of the reciprocal dimension of business. Everyone understands it's in their own interest to help other people. One day these people may be able to help you. Business people are disposed to help, and will gladly do so, especially if it's easy. Believe it or not, they're particularly happy to help someone get a job. For one thing, they're sympathetic because they've been through the process themselves. They also understand they're not only doing you a big favor, they're alerting the HR department to a great candidate. Both parties will feel indebted.

Information is the most commonly traded commodity in business. It could be information about business opportunities, business trends, openings and people looking for jobs, or gossip about who's up and who's down. These are just a few of the topics that are regularly discussed in business settings. When you ask for information, it's easy and low-cost for someone to pass it along.

You're definitely going to be interested in any information your network can provide about the job market. You'll also want to learn about different industries and different types of work. You might want input on specific questions that arise during the search process, including recommendations for how to improve your resume.

When a company hires you, they're making a bet. They're wagering that you'll help their company grow. Making a new hire is an important decision for a company. They don't want to waste their time and money on someone who can't do the job and won't fit into their organization. Because they're taking a risk with monetary consequences, they want as much information as possible about job candidates. Endorsements and suggestions from trusted friends and colleagues will be given more weight if the people making these recommendations are in their network. Therefore, you want as many people as possible in your network.

Despite our dependence on electronic connections, job search requires personal connections—lots of them.

Cultivating Your Network

It's easy to cultivate a business network. Start by listing the names of friends and relatives. If you have easy access to their phone numbers and email addresses you can include those, or you can add them later. Don't let the search for specific contact information distract you from adding more names to your list. Next, identify people who fall under the category "acquaintance." Now think back to college, high school, and even elementary school. Make a list of these names, as well as co-workers from any past employment.

If you are hesitant about starting this process, remember the 30-minute project described earlier. You could even break it down into three 10-minute projects if that's easier. First, list your close friends. On day two, write down the names of current acquaintances. On the third day, search your memory for people from your early years in school. It's that easy.

The prerequisites for "knowing someone" are very low. You don't have to be familiar with any details about these individuals. You don't even have to know their full name. They can still make your list, as long as you remember where you met them, or how they're connected with your distant relative. In time, you'll gather complete names and contact information.

What is your reaction to the list you've created? Are you surprised by who made the list? You should have at least 30–50 possible names. As your list continues to evolve, you'll think of even more people. Plus, the people in your network will suggest names from their contact lists.

Step two involves linking each name to their biographical information. Gathering these facts can be tedious, but you can accumulate this data over time. Here are a few of the things you'll want to know about each person:

1. Email address
2. Phone number
3. Mailing address
4. Type of work
5. Current employer
6. Past employers
7. Name of contact that referred you

Now rate the strength of your connection with each person using a rating scale such as: 1 (know them extremely well); 2 (know moderately well); 3 (have met briefly or know indirectly). With people rated at 2 or 3, include some information about the conditions under which you met. The people with a rating of 1 will be very useful, but the people ranked 2 or 3 will also be extremely useful. Although your connection is weak, these people are important because they add breadth, extending your network out in new directions and into new job markets.

The people in the 2 and 3 categories represent a rich source of potential contacts. While the list of your close friends is limited, you can indefinitely expand the list of people in the 2 and 3 categories. A multiplier effect occurs when you add each new person to your network. Every name represents another entire network. The law of large numbers definitely holds true in networking. The more people you contact, the more likely you'll connect with the right person—the individual who'll offer you a job.

Step 3 involves contacting each of these people. Your minimum goal is to reestablish your relationship, and make them aware you're looking for work. Let them know you'd appreciate any assistance. You may be able to use a version of your elevator pitch (Chapter 15) to structure discussions or email messages with these new contacts.

Expanding Your Network

One simple way to expand your network is to comb your memory for names and faces. Include everyone, even contacts outside the business world. Your Aunt Margaret (a stay-at-home mother) undoubtedly knows many people in business. She might be willing to make a few calls on your behalf, and tap her network of friends and business connections.

Keep jogging your memory. Recall any clubs from college. Try to recall any members of your athletic teams, recreational groups, community service or religious organizations. If you've ever worked part time, jot down the name of your employer and any co-workers. Scan your mind for visual images, and then try to link the face with a name. The Internet (including Facebook) can yield an unexpected windfall of biographical and contact information.

The single best way to expand your group of contacts is to ask people: "Do you have any friends or acquaintances I might call about possible jobs in the healthcare industry?" Obviously, you'll insert the name of the industry or work function that suits your situation. By asking this one simple question, you'll greatly expand the size and scope of your list.

As your search narrows, your questions will become more focused. For example, "Do you know anyone in instructional design at HP?" You don't want to become a pest, or waste people's time. Craft your questions carefully before making any calls. Be selective. Don't send mass emails that litter people's inbox with information that isn't directly relevant to them. When you do contact someone, make it personal. "To Whom It May Concern" is a guaranteed dead end.

Timing is critical. Check in with your network on a regular basis. While you don't want to be a nuisance, it's essential to maintain some type of link with each person in your network. Circumstances are constantly changing. The person you almost scratched off your list last week might have learned of a job opening at their brother's company. If they just recently read an email from you, something might click and they'll give you a call. Send news about your job search, or email a brief quip about a mutual friend. Don't send jokes, chain letters, or cute photos of animals.

Meeting new people is the ideal way to expand your network. As a graduate student you are at a slight disadvantage. Most of your life is centered around the same small group of students and professors. Business people have innumerable opportunities to meet new people—co-workers, colleagues within the industry, and customers. If you have a part-time job outside the university, your opportunities will instantly expand.

Despite the constraints of your situation, there are still many ways you can add names to your network. Set a weekly goal to expand your network. You can begin at the lowest level by adding one person a week, and then try to raise your quota. Take advantage of every social event to step outside your small academic circle.

Any party or social gathering is an opportunity to network. The faces you see at weekend parties may be familiar, but keep your eyes and ears alert to newcomers. Make it a point to talk to these people and learn about the type of work they do and the people they know. It may also be possible to network at weddings, bar mitzvahs or other large gatherings.

If you don't already belong to any on- or off-campus clubs, join one. Select a group that focuses on your areas of interest (e.g., the environment, student government or hobbies such as music, drama or film). You don't have to become an active member, but try to attend a few meetings. Sports are also a great way to meet people. Run laps around the track, go to the workout facility on campus, or the local YMCA.

Check with the business school for a schedule of guest lectures and seminars. Plan to arrive 15 minutes early, and stay after the lecture to mingle and meet new people. Instead of eating lunch in your office, or in the nearest food court, scope out a bench in an area where law or business students congregate.

If you're reluctant to meet new people, try your elevator pitch, or ask a few simple questions. Initiating these conversations can be relatively easy. People enjoy talking about themselves. Have your lunch in locations where you can meet new people. The student union is a good place to start. Try talking with someone who's seated alone.

Look for people in their 30s, 40s, and 50s. They may have administrative positions on campus. Use their work as a springboard to generate conversation.

If you're still a bit nervous about approaching strangers, consider this: What if you were involved in a research project that required you to do random man-on-the-street surveys? Would you feel more comfortable if you had a specific mission? Okay. Here's your research assignment: each week, meet at least one new person during lunch, and learn about their work. Keep a log of your results.

The good news: it gets easier. You'll develop a repertoire of questions that get people talking. Any time you're around people, whether you're on public transportation or just waiting in line at the post office, strike up a conversation. You can always find a point of common interest. In addition to expanding your network, you'll meet many interesting people. You'll quickly gain confidence in your ability to talk to all types of individuals. And, as an added benefit, you'll develop an important asset that will be greatly valued in any future job.

Working a Room

When you enter a social setting with the goal of talking to specific people, you're *working the room*. Many business people are highly practiced at this craft. They know who they want to meet. They have a plan for exchanging business cards, and making follow-up appointments. At work, or in a social setting, they make it a point to also do a little business. Whether at a seminar or attending a party, the rewards of "working a room" can be substantial.

Here's how it's done: Prior to the event, create your plan. Will there be opportunities to socialize? Try to identify in advance the names of any people you want to meet. What other kinds of people might be of interest (e.g., people who work at particular companies or in certain industries)? Creating an action plan will increase your confidence and enable you to make the most of the time you spend with any one person. Be ready for a few surprises. The person you circled as "key" might elude you. As you walk to the parking lot, this VIP's car might be right next to yours. As you fumble with your keys, inquire how they enjoyed the event. Since you didn't have an chance to talk during the evening, ask if you could ask them a question now, or if you could follow up with a phone call? These are important opportunities. Take the risk and initiate a conversation.

Let's assume your goal is to become proficient at networking. Where do you stand now? What has been your modus operandi when you attend most social events? Do you hunt for familiar faces, or slink off to the side and hope someone else makes the first move? From this point forward, you can talk with your friends for only so long. Eventually, you must take the initiative and start working the room. If you're still a bit reluctant, ask a friend to provide an introduction to some people in the room.

Your elevator pitch was designed for these situations. Turn the conversation into a dialogue, not a soliloquy. Remember that you're probably not the only person in the room who's networking. Don't dominate the VIP. Give your elevator pitch, ask your questions, and exchange contact information. It's amazing how much you can accomplish in a brief window of time.

If there is someone you're determined to meet—perhaps the featured speaker at a conference—do your research so you can ask informed and thoughtful questions. In the open discussion after the speech, stand by the podium (you could be standing there for several minutes), so you're positioned to extend a hand in greeting, or open the conversation.

As your confidence grows, you'll learn to maximize your networking opportunities during events that involve a meal, or where people are seated around a table. Don't immediately take a seat when the organizer announces, "dinner is served." Identify the people you'd like to sit with, and stay close to them as they find their table. If there is an open seat, politely ask if you might join them. When seats aren't pre-assigned, put yourself in a location that maximizes your opportunities to network.

Networking is the current word for a practice that occurs in all social groups throughout the world. We all need the assistance of others, and we all hope to return their favors.

15

Your Elevator Pitch

Pretend for a moment. You have an 8 A.M. interview at a major downtown corporation and you're very early. You step into an elevator, and plan to visit the top floor and sneak a peek at the executive offices. Just as the elevator door is closing, a distinguished woman steps in. You recognize her immediately. She pushes the button for the 60th floor and says, "Hello." You're suddenly alone with the CEO. What are you going to do? You have her all to yourself. This is the perfect opportunity to introduce yourself and let her know what you have to offer. What do you say?

Although this sounds like a dream, comparable situations arise in everyday life. You come face to face with a key contact, or hiring manager, and have only a few seconds to tell your story. In the business world, the words you speak in this short window are known as your elevator speech or *elevator pitch*. This mini-speech is similar to the iconic situation in which film writers have only a few minutes to pitch an idea.

What to Say?

Most of us feel a little apprehensive when we introduce ourselves to a stranger. Emotions can move into the red zone when you know the person might hold the key to your future. You have only a brief amount of time to make your pitch—20 to 30 seconds. If you don't make a great impression, there won't be a second chance. It's similar to the speed-dating approach to meeting people.

The situations you face won't be as critical as meeting a Fortune 500 CEO, but during your job search you'll meet many people who will have the capacity to help you. In order to expand your network, you'll have to meet a wide range of people, many of them strangers. During most job interviews, you'll be speaking for the first time to someone who could make or break your job prospects. Fortunately, there are three simple ways to neutralize your fears.

Know exactly what you want to say. Make your words appealing to the listener, and deliver the message in a pleasant and respectful manner. This chapter will provide a ground level guide to help you master all three steps. In everyday exchanges, you undoubtedly use these same three elements whenever you meet someone new. Just condense and polish your words, and improve your style and delivery. By following these ground level steps, you'll gain the confidence to shine in these potentially intimidating situations.

Your Script

"Hi. My name's Jerry, and it's a pleasure to meet you." This everyday sentence, when stated with confidence, is a fine place to start. People sometimes make the error of mumbling when they introduce themselves. You want the person to remember your name, so pronounce it clearly and at full volume. If more than two people ask you to repeat your name, that's a critical warning. You need to enunciate your words and speak loud enough for people to hear.

Sometimes it's helpful to repeat your name right up front, "I'm Jerry, that's Jerry with a J. What's your name?" Repeating your name may sound a little forced, but your goal is to make it clear and memorable. They'll probably smile and respond, "Hi Jerry with a J. I'm Peter with a P."

Given the potential time constraint, you might skip right from your name to some biographical information about yourself, "Hi my name's Jerry and I'm a writer (researcher, archivist, graphic designer, educator, etc.)." Your self-description should convey the skills that are relevant to business.

Usually it's best to mention your skills, or the project you're working on, rather than simply naming your profession. If you tell business people you are a historian, philosopher, psychologist, or linguist, you'll most likely get a blank response. They'll probably say, "Oh, that's interesting." This is a sure sign you're not communicating in words business people understand.

Instead of leading with your profession, start with the strengths that are central to your brand identity. "I'm Ella and I'm researching biomedical issues." Or, "I'm Maggie and my blog focuses on ways to improve health practices." Or, "I'm Jerry and I speak to audiences about ways to overcome resistance to change." A great deal of information can be communicated in five to ten seconds.

Write a draft of your opening statement. It could be three to four sentences. Practice saying it over and over. Keep editing and refining. Imagine saying it to a variety of people. You should be able to describe your key strengths or skills in a single sentence or two. In a setting with other researchers, you might want to stress your research expertise. If the person you've just met has an interest in education, you can highlight your classroom communication skills.

You don't have to tell people you're in graduate school. If you do, you'll also need to explain your career plans. That could take you off message, and squander precious seconds. Focus on your strengths and skills. You could say, "Currently I'm working on a research project at the university." If you tell them you just finished your masters (or Ph.D.) degree, quickly add that the experience greatly improved your analytic (research, writing, etc.) skills. While you are justifiably proud of your thesis, unless it directly relates to business, emphasize the skills you developed while completing the project.

Make It Appealing

The WIIFM principle (pronounced wiff-em) stands for the number-one question in most everyone's mind, *what's in it for me?* With a smile on your face, you can volunteer, "If you ever need help with a writing project, I'll be glad to give you some assistance." Or, "I don't know if you ever need life science information, but feel free to contact me for some tips on searching the web." Here's another way to word your offer, "If you, or a friend, ever have questions about graphic design, I'd be happy to give you some ideas."

You're gracefully and generously volunteering to help them for free. This description of your offer will go through many drafts. Although you begin with three or four sentences, you'll condense it to a single sentence.

You may be thinking, "Why am I offering to do something for nothing when what I really want is a job?" You're basically offering a free sample and indicating that you understand the give-and-take of business. Most people will recognize that your offer contains a hidden sales message. That's okay. It's a good way to get them to like you and to build a business relationship with you.

Very few people will accept your free offer. Instead, it may encourage them to ask you more about your skills and suggest ways you might work together in the future. This would be a great result. Of course, if they take you up on your offer, you'll have to deliver. You can set a time limit on how much you'll provide for free. While you're fulfilling your obligation, you'll become acquainted and possibly put yourself in a position for a job or a referral.

You've given your name and biographical information, and your offer of assistance. Now tell them how they can help you. "I'm interested in meeting people in publishing. Do you know anyone who works in the industry?" Or, "Do you know anyone attending this seminar who works in biotechnology?" If you want to be more explicit, you could say, "I'm looking for a job where I could use my writing skills. Do you know anyone looking for a writer?" A more generic version could be: "I just entered the job market. Do you know anyone who needs a bright, creative, hardworking assistant?"

The format of your message is simple and the actual words are up to you. As you practice, you'll find phrases that are comfortable. At first, this studied approach may seem awkward. When delivered with enthusiasm and a friendly face, its tactical nature will not be apparent. This is your 30-second elevator pitch. You want to make the most of your opportunity to quickly make a connection.

Business people are very accustomed to this kind of exchange. They won't be put off. If they act surprised, they're probably impressed with the precision and polish of your delivery. You're demonstrating your business savvy.

Delivery

Begin with an unforced smile. Your facial expression should make you look friendly and draw people to what you have to say. Pace your words, so you don't overwhelm the listener—think of a gently flowing spring, not a fire hose. Initiate the conversation with a simple question: "There are a lot of people here tonight. Is this a typical turnout?" After exchanging a few words, you can transition into your introduction: "I didn't even introduce myself, I'm Jerry . . ."

Your voice and manner should be amiable and relaxed. Speak slowly, so you appear spontaneous and unhurried. Use voice inflections to highlight key points of information. Pause briefly after each of your three key points. If they don't respond, continue to your next point. Your request for information should be phrased as a question. This type of dialogue is normal and expected in the business world.

You're not delivering a monologue. A nonstop tour through points one, two, and three could be off-putting. Although you will have planned your key points, you don't want to sound scripted or rehearsed. Listen for opportunities to create a dialogue. Your easy questions and slight pauses will encourage participation. You might feel comfortable making a clever response to one of their questions. Humor is almost always welcome. You can then segue back to the next relevant piece of information in your pitch.

Practice, Practice, Practice

Like an actor, your first task is to memorize your lines. You'll probably refine them as you commit them to memory. Next, work on your voice. Identify words you need to enunciate clearly (e.g., your name, your strengths, how committed you are to a business career). Insert pauses to add emphasis, and for spontaneity. Try speaking very slowly and then very fast. Find the pace that feels comfortable, and then work on finding the right volume level.

After the mechanics are in place, begin working on the emotional tone of your delivery. Experiment with varying amounts of emphasis on the key words and phrases. Deliver it first with enthusiasm and then as a matter-of-fact. You'll vary your tone from one person to the next, so it's helpful to practice altering the pitch for each audience.

Next you can work on your mannerisms and your delivery. Find a large mirror and be your own audience. Vary your facial expressions and hand gestures. Experiment until you find the ones that make you appear most confident and relaxed.

Now you're ready to step in front of the camera. If you are like most people, you'd rather record and review your video in private. When you give the call for "action," extend your hand to an imaginary person and begin your remarks. Practice several times, and then select the one you like best for analysis.

Watching yourself on camera is always a little disconcerting. It's natural to focus on the mistakes. Adopt a clinical approach to your video. Start with the basics: enunciation, clarity, volume, points of emphasis, etc. Now analyze the messages you're communicating with your facial expression and manner. Are they aligned with the content? Do you have a smile, or a blank expression on your face when you say you're a positive person? Identify the changes you want to make, practice them several times, and then repeat the video and analysis process. When you're satisfied, invite a trusted friend to give you some feedback on your last take.

The moment you've been waiting for has arrived. You're ready to go "live" with a real audience. It's normal to be nervous and to make mistakes. Don't misinterpret any mistakes as a sign that you can't pull off an elevator pitch. Celebrate the fact that you had the courage to try something entirely new, and in front of strangers. This is a major accomplishment. Learning is part of the process, so let your pitch evolve with each person you meet. Even if you veer off message, you might have had an interesting conversation with the person, and may have collected a business card. The person took an interest in you. That was your goal. You don't have to be perfect.

Your confidence will grow as you learn to vary your delivery and appear more spontaneous. By reacting to your listener's expressions and body language (e.g., friendly–wary, relaxed–tense, open–closed), you'll be able to adjust your comments and manner to match incoming signals. Watch how pros meet and talk to people as they work the room.

Don't be intimidated by people who have a natural ease when talking to strangers. They've done it many times before. They use the same lines over and over. If you followed them, you'd discover they have a large but limited repertoire of opening remarks. They've learned to incorporate a few thoughts from a prior conversation into the current discussion. With experience, you'll gain the same ease and versatility.

In Case of Emergency

Imagine the other person doesn't say anything, but you interpret their puzzled facial expression as, "Who are you and what are you talking about?" This exaggerated fear is just one of the monsters we believe is lurking in the dark. It's not going to happen. At most you'll face someone who is socially awkward and feels uncomfortable. Some people who seem disinterested are actually manifesting their own shyness.

You can use simple questions to move both of you out of the awkward zone. You could try some general business questions.

"How is this economy impacting your work?"
"Do you look for things to improve or stabilize?"

You could ask a question based on a current event such as:

"Is the recent change in oil prices impacting your business?"
"What effect has the election had on your company?"
"Did you hear the president's speech last night? Do you think it will have any impact on the economy?"

Instead of asking questions about the weather, or a sports team, try to get them talking about a current event in relation to business. If you still hit a wall, go back to the weather or the Yankees. Find a graceful way to move on by saying, "Nice meeting you."

Risks = Rewards

Meeting strangers is easier for some people than for others. If you find it challenging, think about the consequences of not being brave, or not talking to any new people. Outsiders are the key to getting a good job. If you rely only on the individuals you already know (most of whom are in academics), it's going to take a much longer time to find work. That's your WIIFM and here's your action plan.

Take it slow, and take small steps. If you're really terrified, begin by just observing. Go to a few social events. You don't have to speak to anyone. By just attending, you're taking the first big step. Of course, if someone does approach you, or you see someone you'd like to meet, you could make an exception to your vow of silence and enter into a conversation.

Even though you may have fears and doubts, you can at least say hello. Don't surrender your life to these negative emotions. Acknowledge these internal feelings, and then bravely take one or two steps in the right direction. People aren't nearly as ferocious as you imagine. Most people welcome the opportunity to make a new acquaintance. You never know which person might be the link to your job.

16

Assets and Liabilities

What qualities do you bring to a business job? The strengths of your brand must be translated into the language of business. Use action verbs to make your talents stand out on your resume. This process of redefining yourself will also be useful on job interviews and in networking discussions. In grad school, your abilities were evaluated in terms of your probable success as a professor. Now reframe your personal resources in the terminology of business.

You can claim several broad categories of resources. You've mastered an academic specialty, and have acquired important research skills. These may or may not be helpful in getting a job. It's more common for grad students who work outside academia to become involved with projects that are partially related to their disciplinary major. They may draw on the theories and research they studied, but more often they rely on the general skills and knowledge they developed in grad school.

In addition, you acquired the analytic and communication abilities required for advanced graduate work. You may have worked in business, or you've probably been a T.A. or a R.A. Add to that, your unique personal attributes and life experiences. All of these will be among the assets you bring to business.

Disciplinary Expertise

The understanding you've gained in an academic specialty has always been a source of pride, and if it has direct applications in business settings, it could lead to a job. Grad students working in scientific, engineering, and technical disciplines can often make an easy transition into business. Some students in the social sciences will also be able to translate their specific expertise into business assignments. Demographers and other applied social scientists can often find work that's related to their specialty. Jobs in marketing, advertising, customer relations, and health practices are good places for social science grad students to start searching.

There are a few, but not as many, beginning positions that require the sophisticated knowledge developed in the arts and humanities. You might be hired by an educational institution or an organization involved with preservation (e.g., museums and historical sites) because of your disciplinary knowledge.

While your specialty may not get you a job, the secondary knowledge associated with your discipline may help you get a foot in the door. It's likely you could be hired because your general field of study is relevant to the company's work. A global company may be interested in a grad student with an understanding of the language and culture of a certain region or country. A pharmaceutical company may be attracted to a grad student with a background in biology or chemistry. This knowledge would add to their qualifications as a sales representative. A firm that is involved with customer service may be drawn to psychology students, on the assumption that they possess good people skills. Technology companies who provide information-search services often hire grad students in the fields of mathematics and statistics.

Getting a job is going to require a realistic assessment of everything you have to offer. You may be disappointed when companies appear to undervalue the breadth and depth of your disciplinary knowledge. This is the way of the world. The differences between the values in academia and business are cut-and-dry. They're interested in what you can do for them—that means 100% business.

Research Skills

The methodological, quantitative and technological skills you developed in graduate school are a definite asset. Businesses, government agencies, and not-for-profit organizations hire large numbers of people to conduct research. You may also be hired because your skills are relevant to certain portions of your job. For example, you may be called on at times to evaluate the research of other companies, or to interpret their data and findings.

Many grad students underestimate the commercial importance of these skills. They compare their level of knowledge against a very high standard—the professors teaching the courses—rather then comparing themselves with the

average business employee. Your skills and experience will appear very sophisticated to many organizations.

Begin by making a list of the research methodologies and laboratory techniques you have mastered. Now record the statistical tests and packages with
which you are familiar. You don't have to use them regularly. List all the statistical tests you can perform and interpret. Some tests that seem elementary to
you, may be just what a company is seeking. If you are skilled at qualitative
research techniques, list these as well (e.g., interviewing, running discussion
groups). Also include any technical equipment you know how to operate. For
example, your ability to operate an MRI machine, or other highly sophisticated
equipment, could make you stand out.

You'll be able to use this list of skills in several places on your resume.
When a resume is optically scanned, key words are identified in an effort to
screen out candidates who lack the minimal skill base. By including these items
on your list, you'll increase your chances of surmounting this hurdle.

Personal Attributes

One of the fundamental laws of interpersonal attraction is that we are drawn to
people who are similar. We seek people who have the same values and life
experiences. Sometimes job interviewers feel an instant connection to graduates from their own alma mater. It's hard to predict which distinctive personal
qualities will connect with an interviewer. It may be that you were raised in the
same region, or that you spent a semester in France. The interviewer may also
play tennis, or belong to the same animal rescue organization.

These secondary personal features are seldom enough to get you a job.
However, if you are otherwise qualified for the position, these distinctive qualities can give you an edge over another candidate. While you can only list a few
of these secondary attributes on your resume, you can insert one or two during
the interview.

During the small talk before the interview, you could reveal a lot about yourself
in only two sentences. "I spent six months in Italy. I not only love the culture, but I
learned to cook and I became a dedicated soccer fan." That reveals multiple possible points of connection. If the interviewer knows Italy, you may receive a smile.
If you're specifically asked about these secondary characteristics, keep your remarks
brief. Find a way to connect an attribute back to business. "Italian cooking is relax-
ing but it reminds me that no one ingredient makes a great dish. It's like teamwork; everyone makes their unique contribution to achieve a great final result."
The linkage can be tenuous, but it shows that your prime focus is always work.

Pay careful attention to any personal information revealed by the interviewer. Listen for any points of similarity. Even the most elementary things:
where you were raised, similarities in your appearance (e.g., you're both tall,
redheaded, etc.). These can become the basis for establishing another linkage.
Pictures, artwork, and objects in a person's office give clues about their personal life. (Check to make sure the interview is being held in *their* office before
you compliment their family photos.) A brief comment or question may create
another point of connection.

General Traits

Academicians prize intellectual and analytic brilliance on their own merit,
while business people regard analytic ability as a tool to solve practical problems and get results. Try recasting your general characteristics in the language
of business. As discussed in Chapter 1, graduate students have an impressive
list of attributes. While most employers will assume you are a good thinker,
you'll want to recast these abilities in business terminology. Discuss how your
skills enable you to solve problems and develop innovative solutions. Make
certain to stress your capacity to learn quickly. This is important in any new
position, but it's critical for most grad students because they lack work experience. Because you can learn quickly, this will shorten the time it normally takes
new hires to become productive contributors. Your writing and speaking skills
indicate your ability to communicate clearly in team situations.

Another set of dimensions grad students often take for granted, but
employers value, are maturity, drive, and sense of responsibility. You're older
than the typical college graduate. You had to be very self-directed in your
research. As a teaching assistant, you were in a position of responsibility and
authority. You can also point to your capacity for hard work. Any setbacks on a
research project demonstrate your perseverance. You also know how to meet
deadlines and turn in work that is error-free.

Under the guidance of a major professor, you learned to follow instructions
and to accomplish goals with very little direction or supervision. If you worked in
a research group or laboratory, you learned to work effectively as a team member.
Research also requires precision and error-free performance. Because there are
many unknowns in research, you acquired the ability to create innovative solutions and achieve your goals despite unexpected obstacles. You have also learned
how to gain the cooperation of people (i.e., professors, as well as peers).

These traits are highly valued in business. Every company seeks employees
who can learn quickly and then function independently. They want individuals

who are highly motivated, goal oriented, and capable of following established procedures and meeting deadlines. They also want people who think outside the box and who are innovative. (Of course, the ideal employee must also abide by established practices and follow instructions.) Another trait you've developed is the ability to work effectively with individuals from diverse backgrounds.

Do these attributes describe you? Can you see how your qualifications match the needs of the business world? You may lack work experience but you can cast your characteristics in terms that match the mindset of business people.

Liabilities

While you bring a myriad of assets to the job market, the fact that you're attending graduate school could raise a red flag for potential employers. They'll probably have questions about your commitment and readiness to work in business. Your challenge will be to convince skeptical employers that your are not just highly qualified, but that you'll also be a highly motivated employee. You must make them know you've left the ivory tower behind forever. You want them to feel your complete commitment to a career in business.

Loyalty is highly prized in the business world. Employers may fear you will leave after a few months, if you learn of a better job elsewhere. Employers are making a personal investment in hiring and training you. They want to be certain you will remain for several years, so they can get a fair return on their investment. Let them know you want to work for a company where you can learn and grow for many years. Your years of commitment to grad school are ample testimony of how long and hard you're willing to work.

Your attitude could also be a concern. Once you get on the job, will you feel overqualified and act like the work is beneath you? Their worst fear is that you will be condescending to your co-workers, and cause unnecessary problems. You want to emphasize that you're aware how much you have to learn. You love to learn. You'll be grateful for all the knowledge you'll acquire on the job. Express admiration for people who have been successful in business, and indicate you are certain they have a great deal to teach you. Without overstating your case, make it clear you firmly believe you'll work effectively with fellow employees.

An employer may also worry that you'll become disillusioned with business. You may return to academics. If you become disenchanted, your motivation will drop and the quantity and quality of your performance will suffer. You could alienate customers. Your co-workers will resent that you aren't pulling your fair share of the workload. Because of these concerns, it's important to restate the finality of your decision to leave academics.

Emphasize the reasons you left academics, and state that you'll never go back. Express your excitement at building a successful career in business. Enumerate the specific things about the company, the industry, and the work that perfectly match your abilities and goals. Make the interviewer feel your enthusiasm.

Your lack of specific business experience is another major weakness. Don't try to convince the interviewer that it doesn't matter (remember your skepticism toward the grad school applicant who was blasé about her lack of research experience.). You can briefly acknowledge the problem, but then stress how hard you're prepared to work to overcome this deficiency. Reiterate your capacity to learn quickly and cite examples.

No job candidate is 100% perfect, no matter how highly qualified. The capacity to acknowledge a weakness is viewed as a strength, especially when accompanied by a strategy to overcome any deficiency. This honesty shows maturity and character. On balance, your strengths far outweigh your liabilities. You can therefore speak with confidence about the many reasons why you are the best person for the job.

17

Do You Need Another Degree?

Nooo! Perhaps that answer is a bit over the top but the reality is, you can get a job now. You already have the ability and maturity to get a good job. Your research, teaching, and communication skills make you highly desirable. And, you've grown as a person during grad school, which gives you an important edge over undergrads who are also looking for their first jobs.

It will take time to find a job, and you'll encounter many barriers along the way. These impediments can be emotionally difficult for grad students who are accustomed to achieving their goals. It's tempting to escape the demands and uncertainties of the job search by switching over to something you're very good at—education. When you're discouraged, enrolling in a fulltime, multiyear degree or certification program that promises a job can sound appealing.

Don't ever make important decisions when you're down in the doldrums. Let's examine the advantages and disadvantages of getting another degree. Since the default position of this book is not to encourage another degree at this time, we'll first examine the disadvantages before taking up the advantages.

Disadvantages

The first reason to stay in the job market is that you're already qualified for many beginning positions. Your work resume may be thin, but you have multiple talents and you're hardworking. Someone will give you an opportunity, and when they do, you'll prove your worth.

Look at the financial implications of another year or two of education. Think of all the money you could earn if you were employed; your total compensation package (salary, bonuses, and fringe benefits) would be sizeable. But instead of tens of thousands of dollars coming into your accounts, your money will be going out. You'll have more tuition fees and related expenses. These debts will be accumulating interest that you'll have to pay in the future.

Tuition and income would be less a concern if you received a fellowship or assistantship, but funding is scarce in master's level and certificate programs. When you add your annual expenses to the compensation you could be receiving, it won't take long before you approach $100,000 per annum that is in the red, not the black. Even if you eventually get a great job, it could take a decade to make up all that money.

If you do decide to get another degree, can you be guaranteed it will lead to satisfying employment? Will you get a job you really like? Deciding on the industry and type of work you want to pursue is difficult when you have limited work experience. That's the reason this book endorses the strategy of refining your career path once you are in the business world.

With actual work experiences and the knowledge you'll gain about new job possibilities, you'll be in a better position to decide what you want for your life's work. Since you don't have much experience, your decision to earn another degree is based on very limited information. You may be starting on a career track for the wrong reasons.

How can you be certain this new degree or certificate will lead to a job? No doubt the brochures and the program counselors will tout their success in placing students. It may sound good, but you also need to be a little skeptical. They may be called counselors, but they're also recruiters. Don't be satisfied with glowing examples of one or two graduates who received great jobs in the last few years.

Ask if they have quantitative figures on their job placement record during the past five years. They should have this type of data, and they should be able to identify the jobs and institutions where their graduates were placed. Also, ask what percentage of students who start the program actually complete their degrees. A few people always drop out of any degree program. If more than 20% do not finish their degrees, it suggests they may have become disenchanted with the program and its promises.

What about a Masters of Business Administration? In the last few decades, the MBA degree has been portrayed as an automatic entry pass to a high-flying career in business. The MBAs who make headlines with their extraordinary job offers usually had several years of business experience (that's a requirement for entry to the best business programs) and they graduated from a highly ranked business school.

If you are accepted to one of the top 10, or even one of the top 20 business schools in the country—go for it. Investing in another two years will most likely have a significant effect on your income. Getting an MBA from a lesser school, especially if you don't have much work experience, is unlikely to dramatically increase your job prospects. It will help you get interviews, but the jobs you'll be offered won't have significantly higher salaries than what you could earn right now.

The question of whether you need another degree is an emphatic "no." "No" to earning more degrees, but "yes" to more education. A few more skills will be a significant addition to your resume. Do you need to enroll in a fulltime program to gain that knowledge? As described earlier, many computer software skills and other business-related knowledge can be acquired through seminars that require much less time and money than a fulltime program.

Finally, how will you feel about yourself during the two years you spend working on another degree? No doubt you'll feel productive because you have a clear goal and a good chance of successful employment. But, there will be times when you'll count the time passing and wonder why you don't have real income like other people your age. After a while, you'll get tired of living like a student. Not having enough money to enjoy some of the small luxuries of life can become frustrating, and even embarrassing. You may also have doubts about whether you really want to go down the career track promised by the degree program. These may be the normal misgivings everyone experiences about a new endeavor, or you may feel a deeper uncertainty because your decision was based on erroneous information.

Advantages

"Yes" to a degree if it is absolutely essential for entry into a professional career you feel passionate about. Obviously, you'll need an M.D. if you want to become a physician, and a J.D. if you've decided to become an attorney. Many careers in medicine (e.g., physical therapist, nursing, physician's assistant, and technical specialties) require a degree, or the completion of a certificate program. There are several other professions where a degree, or certificate, is mandatory (e.g., C.P.A., financial planner, and professional social worker).

Primary and secondary education usually requires a state teaching certificate, but often you can get a temporary exemption. You can begin teaching and complete the certification courses on weekends or online. It's also possible to begin teaching and to complete a Masters of Education degree online, from an accredited university or college. You can be earning an income while using a low-cost mechanism to become certified. This certificate will enable you to move up several levels on the school district's salary schedule.

The other main advantage of enrolling in a fulltime multiyear program may be psychological. You will have a feeling of certainty about what you are going to do with your business life. A degree program can be especially comforting when people ask about your career plans. It sounds much better to say you are working on a degree or certificate, than to say you're still unemployed and searching for a job.

Deciding

Searching for a job is going to be hard work. There will be hurdles, obstructions, and failures. You will be tempted to find a quick escape from these negative emotions. When you're feeling discouraged, it's easy to be convinced that another degree is the solution to all your problems. Maybe it is, but it's also likely that you are rationalizing a plan that will enable you to temporarily avoid unpleasant realities.

Is this alternative path a real solution, or just a rationalization? That question is difficult to answer. If you want a particular job, and there is an extremely high probability that the degree will lead to this well-paying job, then it's a realistic option. If you're uncertain about the career you want, then you need to be skeptical of your decision. As an experienced job recruiter said, "Graduate school is the worst place to discover what you want to do."

Take a vacation for a few days from the job search process. Get completely away from all the pressure and stress. Spend some time with your friends, and get out into nature. Clear your head, and then come back to the search process. Everything will seem more doable.

Any time you're perplexed about a decision, it's good to get an outsider's perspective. Seek the counsel of an experienced advisor in your network. Explain everything you've learned about the new degree program. Lay out your situation in detail, and honestly describe both the pros and the cons. Document all the things you have done to locate a job. Give your advisor time to consider the options, and then listen to his or her opinion with an open mind.

If you feel hesitant to seek advice, that's usually a warning. It probably signals the fear that your advisor will not agree with the decision you've already made. Your hesitance to talk about your choice indicates that you definitely need an independent perspective. Seek out friends and advisors who not only care about you, but will also bring an experienced and open mind to the discussion. They may agree with your goals, but they may recommend a different path.

Ultimately, it's your career—the choice is yours alone.

18

Graduate Student Resumes

A high score on the GRE will not guarantee your admission to a graduate program, but a low score might disqualify you. In the same way, your resume alone won't get you a job, but it can eliminate you from consideration. It's not just the content of your resume that it is judged. The style and appearance are equally important.

Some grad students anticipate writing their resume with almost as much trepidation as they had about completing a dissertation. In truth, there is nothing to fear. Your resume, like your CV, is a brief description of what you have done. It's only one page in length and follows a standard format. Study the example given below. You can find other examples of resumes at JobsA2B.com and other web sites.

Here are some general observations and warnings about resumes before getting down to ground level. You can create your own resume. Most people who pay someone to prepare their resume, or purchase a software package, end up dissatisfied. At best, the product you get back is a first draft that will require extensive editing. These online companies invariably use a chronological format, which does not work well for people with limited work experience. Follow the guidelines below and put it together yourself.

Many people are tempted to falsify the information on their resume. Don't do it. It's wrong, and with the current access to personal information on the web, you'll probably get caught. Although you never want to give information that is false, it is common practice to emphasize certain parts of your past and ignore others. Similarly, always choose the wording that puts your achievements in the most favorable light. This is your advertisement, so tell the world how fabulous you are.

Despite the sonnet-like restrictions on business resumes, a good resume is more a work of art than a rule-bound creation. You'll show your resume to many people, and get all kinds of feedback. Like a piece of art, a "good" resume is a matter of judgment, so expect different evaluations. Use the following recommendations as a point of departure and then adapt your resume accordingly.

Content

The greatest difference between a CV and a resume is the critical content. A CV highlights your publication record and grants. Academicians are interested in your past scholarship because it's a good predictor of future productivity.

Are you sitting down? You probably shouldn't list these publications or grants on your resume. They are major achievements, and you should be proud of them. It's not that they're unimportant. They link you, however, to the academic sphere, which can cause interviewers to doubt your commitment to business. You can mention them in the interview if you are asked. Otherwise, concentrate on what's important in the business world.

Business people are concerned with your work-related activities because these are the best indicators of your potential for success. You would only list your publications if you were applying for a research-related job. Instead, you're going to describe how the strengths (remember your brand) you've developed through your life experiences can be of value to a company. Before getting into a detailed discussion of the content of your resume, let's begin by looking at the structure and graphic format from the top.

Your name (in a larger font) and contact information will be centered at the top of the page. Since any interested employers will respond to your resume by phone or via email, you don't have to include your mailing address, especially if it's temporary. If you want to protect your mailing address, don't include your number or street. You can simply use the name of your city without a zip code. Illustration 2 presents a sample resume. You'll find more at JobsA2B. com and on the web.

It's often recommended that you list your job objective in a single sentence. If you state your objective too specifically, however, you may exclude yourself from other jobs in the company. Your resume may go to a human resources hiring director hoping to fill several different jobs. You may not be the ideal candidate for the job to which you applied, but you might be perfect for another opening.

Katherine A. Lockwood

Wilshire Boulevard
Los Angeles, California
Cell: (310) 550-2345
klockwood@yahoo.com

EDUCATION:

MICHIGAN STATE UNIVERSITY East Lansing, MI
Bachelor of Science, Chemistry, 2006
HONORS: Summa Cum Laude

UNIVERSITY OF SOUTHERN CALIFORNIA
Master of Science, Neuro-Science, 2009
NIH Scholarship 3 years

STRENGTHS:

Critical Thinking

- Proposed a framework to integrate conflicting empirical results
- Analyzed the root cause of a mechanical problem saving $4K
- Published paper summarizing the result of 37 prior papers

Innovative

- Developed a new methodology to improve self report health data
- Saved $10k by adapting an old machine to perform new services
- Created a new education module on social networking saving $5K

Hard working

- Completed a fMRI study with 16 subjects in just two weeks
- Co-authored a record of 3 research articles in one year
- Worked evenings and weekends to raise $8K in charity funds

LANGUAGES: Spanish fluent; Portuguese conversational

ACTIVITIES: FEMA certified disaster manager; Red Cross volunteer; Math tutor

HOBBIES: Rock climbing; Ballroom dancing; Chinese and Indian cooking

COMPUTER SKILLS: Microsoft Office; SPSS; LexisNexis; Quick Books; Vista, Linux, Mac

FIGURE 18.1

Conversely, if you state your goals too generally ("Seeking a challenging position in which I can use my creative abilities"), it can sound like a greeting card, and you'll give the impression of being naïve. An alternative is to state your work objective in a cover letter rather than on the resume. This will enable you to tailor the letter to a particular company and will also free several lines on your one-page resume.

Another recommendation is to put the equivalent of an executive summary above the more detailed description of your past accomplishments. While summaries are almost always useful to the reader, they can take up a large portion of real estate on that single page. On the other hand, if you don't have a great many business-related achievements, then a summary may work to your benefit.

Next will be the section that outlines your education. List the name of your undergraduate university or college, and the degree you earned, the year you graduated, and any academic honors. Except for graduating seniors, adults don't include their GPA. The fact that you went on to grad school implies a strong undergraduate track record. Do not include specific courses but, it is fine to list any honors.

Strengths

Resumes utilize one of two basic strategies for listing your accomplishments and outstanding attributes. One approach is to outline your job experiences in *chronological* order starting with the most recent. State the company name, the title describing the kind of work you performed, and your *years* of employment (i.e., write "2010" rather than "June–August 2010"). Bullet points are then used to highlight significant achievements or responsibilities. Use action verbs (lists of action verbs are widely available online) and quantified results to dramatize your accomplishments. The chronological strategy is the best approach if you have at least two significant work experiences in the business world.

If you don't have much business experience, or your only paid work was as a teaching or research assistant, a *functional* style of resume can be more effective. Instead of listing your past work experiences, you can identify three or four strengths and use bullet points to describe how you've used these strengths. If you have any business experience, you can site a specific accomplishment beneath a strength. If innovation is a strength, you might state: "Developed a Facebook marketing page for Acme Company."

There are many ways you can provide behavioral examples of your strengths by drawing on your experiences as a T.A. or R.A. Begin by listing the activities you performed in your teaching assistantships. Here are some duties that may be applicable:

- Teaching a class session
- Leading discussion or review sessions
- Tutoring individual students
- Advising individual students
- Conducting research and gathering materials for a professor's lectures
- Managing the course website
- Constructing tests and monitoring exams
- Grading examinations and evaluating performance

- Recording and maintaining class records
- Protecting students' personal information
- Handling "customer" complaints about a professor
- Improving student satisfaction by teaming with the professor and others
- Supervising, scheduling, and delegating responsibility to associates

This last item only applies if you were the head T.A. and had additional managerial duties over other T.A.s.

Now make a list of any duties you had as a research assistant, such as:

- Designing research projects and the associated techniques
- Conducting research using specific methodologies and equipment
- Analyzing the empirical data using specific statistical tests and software
- Locating and examining archival information and databases
- Utilizing technologies and equipment
- Writing research reports and assisting in writing grant proposals
- Teaming with colleagues to coordinate activities
- Supervising and guiding the performance of other researchers

Again, the last item would only apply if you did indeed manage the activities of people who worked on the project. It doesn't matter if the people were other grad students, or unpaid undergraduate volunteers. On your resume, this could be used to support your strengths in teamwork or leadership: "managed the performance of a 5-member team." Citing such behavior is an example of an honest, but slightly inflated resume language. Ideally, you'll be able to add even more items to these two lists.

Compare these lists with your top five strengths. Pick a strength and cite specific work experiences in which you utilized your strength. Here are some examples to illustrate how to adapt this process to your resume. Once you organize a few strengths it'll get easier.

People Skills

- Resolved team conflicts to complete X project on time

- Motivated a team to continue a 6-month research project

- Mediated 5 serious complaints about a course instructor

- Organized volunteers to raise $5K for Hurricane Katrina victims

Use an action verb to start each point. Quantify bullet points by including numbers adds credibility. Although it won't always be possible, try to edit your bullet point to fit on one line (it's easier to read). If most of your examples are drawn from your work as a T.A. or R.A., you don't want to remind readers of your narrow range of experience. Omit the name of the university or the course title. If you have other work experience, name the organization involved. As in the last bullet-point example above, you can also draw from activities in your personal life. Here are more illustrations.

Innovative

- Developed a methodology to improve self-report health data
- Saved $10k by adapting existing equipment to perform new tasks
- Created an education module on social networking saving $5K
- Invented a fund raising procedure that increased donations by 10%

Hard working

- Completed a fMRI study with 16 subjects in just 2 weeks
- Co-authored a record of 5 research articles in one year
- Managed a project during supervisor's 3 month leave
- Worked evenings and weekends to raise charity funds

Leadership

- Lead a 4-person team during a two-week field research project
- Helped students organize voluntary study groups for major exams
- Successfully applied for $10K for a student networking project
- Headed a 3-person group that participated in faculty meetings
- Voted captain of H.S. volleyball team as a junior

Critical Thinking

- Proposed a framework to integrate conflicting empirical results
- Analyzed the root cause of a mechanical problem, saving $4K
- Published a paper summarizing the result of 37 prior studies
- Negotiated a space utilization conflict between two professors

Write these descriptions of your top five strengths and then tailor each resume to the particular job by selecting the three strengths that are most relevant. If you're applying for a position in marketing and advertising, you might emphasize your strength in innovation. But, if the job involved marketing *research,* you should include your quantitative and research strengths instead.

You can use illustrations from earlier in your life, not just grad school. The prior example of raising money for charity occurred during high school. Systematically think of examples from all aspects of your life that could document your strengths. Show each draft of your resume to people in your network for their suggestions and editorial recommendations. Be aware. These are personal judgments and may be contradictory. You'll make the final decision about how to utilize their advice. Resumes are always being revised, so you can continue to improve your bullet point examples.

The next section might best be called "quirky things about me," but it usually goes under titles such as: activities, interests, involvements, and athletics. This is where you include club and organization memberships, offices you've held, sports teams, recreational activities and hobbies. For example:

Involvements: National Honor Society; officer of a fraternity or sorority

Activities: Red Cross volunteer and blood donor; math tutor

Athletics: member of national Ultimate Frisbee team; H.S. swim team

Hobbies: rock climbing, ballroom dancing, Chinese and Indian cooking, watercolor painting

These personal qualities illustrate more than your past accomplishments, or that you're well rounded. They can serve as a hot-button that grabs an interviewer's attention. Perhaps the interviewer was also a swimmer and she understands the dedication required in the sport. Rock climbing might catch the eye of a firm that wants risk takers. Of course, it might be a red flag warning to a conservative financial institution, so carefully edit the information on the resume to fit each company.

Avoid listing *travel* and *reading* among your hobbies. Everyone travels and everyone reads, so this doesn't make you distinctive. But if you've traveled extensively in Africa, or you read the journal *Foreign Affairs,* these could be considered unique attributes and they could attract an organization involved with global issues. By including a particular cuisine, your interest in cooking might also suggests a strong international orientation.

The final section on your resume is a basket category that is used to list specific skills and accomplishments. Sometimes this is called *Skills* or *Additional Information* and it might look like this:

Computer: Microsoft Office, LexisNexis, Quicken, Vista, Linux, Mac

Languages: Spanish, fluent; German, read and translate

Skill Sets: Project management, fMRI recording, FEMA certified disaster manager, notary, SPHR

Feel free to list all potentially relevant skills, so the scanner doesn't discard your resume. Be certain to replicate the language and buzzwords used in the job description or advertisement. Otherwise, the scanner will probably eliminate you from consideration.

This section can be very dense and doesn't have to be visually appealing. You don't need to use bullet points or action verbs. Your lists don't have to fit on one line. After you pass this electronic evaluation of minimum qualifications, the interviewer will hunt for the skills that have particular importance in this job.

Format

While a CV can be many pages in length (sometimes longer is better), your resume will be one, and only one page. Unless you are applying for a position as a graphic artist, your resume should be plain vanilla. Use white paper, a standard font and size, normal margins, and black ink. This is what people expect, and when you follow these guidelines it gives them confidence that you understand business etiquette.

The space limitations of a resume often come in conflict with the natural desire to fill all the space with more information about your attributes. People have tried innumerable ways to get as many words as possible on to one page. Some people stretch the margins to the edge of the page. Don't do it. Leave at least one inch around all sides. Other people try to finesse the guidelines by decreasing the size of the printing font. Is it easy to read the following line?

Here's size 12 font. This is size 11 font. Here's size 10 font. This is size 9 font. Here's size 8 font.

Now picture someone who has already reviewed 50 resumes in the last 20 minutes and has at least 50 more to go. If you do the math, it's clear that on the first evaluation, most resumes receive less than 30 seconds of attention. Actually many get only 5 or 10 seconds, because the reviewer spent several extra minutes on an exceptional resume. Even with the many great accomplishments listed on your resume, a small font size will literally minimize your resume and possibly annoy a harried reader. Stick with size 12, and at the minimum, size 11. Use a font with a conventional type face.

Always use high quality bond paper for your resume. An office supply store can advise you on the best papers for resumes. Purchase 8 ½ x 11 envelopes so you can mail your resume flat. Resumes never look as impressive when they're folded.

Visual appeal is especially important to someone who is reviewing 100 resumes in less than an hour. Would you be more likely to read a page that was dense with black type, or one that had a fair amount of white space? Negative space can be an asset. People will spend more time with a resume that is inviting to the eyes. Don't clutter your resume with too many words. Identify the portions of your resume that seem congested, and find a way to condense and combine items.

Because there is a surfeit of applicants for most job openings, recruiters often look for small errors to disqualify applicants. Spelling and grammar mistakes could drastically lower your rating. Have multiple people check and recheck your resume. Some recruiters vigilantly hunt for inconsistencies. If the dates for jobs and degrees aren't in sync, it will raise suspicion. If the title and description of a past job sounds much more responsible than your present job, alarm bells will go off. You don't want the interviewer to wonder: Why did he take such a giant step down? Or, did he hyperinflate the responsibilities associated with the prior position? These kinds of inconsistencies suggest dishonesty, and they cast suspicion over the entire resume. Tell the truth.

In academia, it is common to give the names and addresses of your references. You are often instructed to have your references send letters in conjunction with your CV. This is not accepted practice in business. Don't list your references and don't include the sentence, "References available upon request." It is assumed that you will be able to provide references if they request them. If you have a VIP as a reference, mention the name in your cover letter, not in your resume.

The Cover Letter

Whether you submit your resume electronically or via the U.S. Postal Service, your cover letter is a crucial element of your application. Interviewers may first look at your resume, and if you seem interesting, they'll go back and carefully read your cover letter. Many examples of cover letters can be found online.

Use high quality bond paper and envelopes. Once again, white is the preferred color. The letter should fit on one page and contain 3–4 paragraphs. Ideally the opening salutation references a specific person that you will address by name. If you don't have a name, the letter is addressed to "Dear Hiring Manager" or "Dear Recruiter." Never send it To Whom It May Concern. The content of each letter should be tailored to the job and the company. Cover letters are usually included as an attachment on electronic submissions.

The format is fairly simple. In paragraph one you describe (in the company's words) the specific position to which you are applying. Explain how you learned about the opening. If someone inside the company told you about the job, definitely include their name and title. If they are sufficiently important, use the name in the first sentence. "John Doe, the Vice President of Marketing at Acme Inc., recommended that I apply for the job opening in..."

Use the second paragraph to convey why the job has so much appeal. Begin by praising the best features of the company. This will show that you've done your research and that you sincerely want the job. If many aspects of the company and job appeal to you, carefully condense the message to three or four sentences.

Next, describe how two of your strengths would benefit the company. You'll define your strengths in detail on your resume. For the cover letter, simply name the strength and suggest how it could help the organization move forward. This must be accomplished in a few sentences, and you should not use bullet points in your letter.

In the final paragraph, describe what you hope will happen next. Suggest that you'd like to set up a meeting. Or, indicate that if you haven't received a reply within two weeks you'll contact the company (to make sure they received your materials) and inquire about a possible meeting.

The word "sincerely" is a good closing salutation. Type your name in full and leave room above it for a handwritten signature in dark ink. Some people include a post script. Since these letters are printed however, post scripts appear contrived. If you have an extremely *vital* message, you can include a very brief handwritten post script. Several people should absolutely read the letter for errors and typos before you sign and send it to the company.

Thank-You Notes

This may seem reminiscent of 18th century Europe, but interviewing is a formal process, so you need to follow an interview with a thank you note. It should be handwritten, contain 3–7 sentences, and be mailed within 24–36 hours of the interview. If your handwriting is not an asset, then print the note on the computer. Use high quality note paper or cards and envelopes. The card should be simple and plain. Avoid floral displays or animals, no matter how cute.

There are several ways you can add to the substance of your note. Take a few minutes immediately after the meeting to privately outline the key aspects of the interview. You'll be surprised how many elements you'll remember.

Start with the interviewer's name. Make sure to spell it correctly. Check their business card (that you asked for). Use their title on the envelope. In the first sentence, express your gratitude and mention your increased interest in the position. In the next sentence mention a specific thing the interviewer said that was especially helpful. Next, briefly describe the key reason (probably connected to one of your strengths) you are the ideal candidate for the job. Your final line restates your gratitude, and expresses your desire to hear back from them soon.

Date

Dear Mr. Smith,

    Thank you for a most enjoyable meeting today. When you explained how this job contributes to your company's overall marketing and sales strategy, I was convinced - this is the job for me. My research experiences, combined with my interpersonal skills are a perfect fit for the job. These skills will enable me to make an immediate contribution.

    Again, thank you for your time and consideration. I look forward to hearing from you within ten days.

Sincerely,

Jane Doe

Jane Doe

FIGURE 18.2

SECTION IV

Landing Your Job

19

Searching For Your Job

Rate each search tactic with this scale: 1   2   3   4   5   6   7

Write your number on the blank line.   Passive   Active

For example: __1__Sitting at home hoping someone calls with a job offer

____Posting your resume on your web site

____Searching major job web sites

____Searching for jobs on a company's web site

____Submitting a resume in response to a posted job opening

____Submitting an unsolicited resume to a company

____Researching industries and companies

____Sending an update of your search process to your network

____Establishing a networking link with people at social gatherings

____Attending a job fair on campus

____Using the services at the university's career center

____Hiring an online firm to create your resume and cover letter

____Attending a networking meeting

____Forming a Search and Assist group

___Going early to a business seminar to meet new people

___Placing a phone call to a company to inquire about job openings

___Using your network to find someone currently working at a company

___Walking into a company and inquiring about an opening

Using your numeric ratings, imagine person A who relies *exclusively* on the job search tactics you rated as a 1, 2, or 3. Now picture candidate B who relies *primarily* on the job search tactics you rated as 5, 6, or 7. Assuming they both have comparable resumes, who will get a job faster?

Utilizing active job search practices will secure a position more quickly than relying on passive search tactics. You must seriously consider this question. Do you want to wait, or would you rather have a job as soon as possible? You can accelerate how quickly you earn a salary by utilizing active search practices. Some people begin with the more passive techniques, but in time they adopt a more active approach.

When used to excess, some of the active search tactics can be executed in such a way as to offend and alienate. Presumably, you'll use good judgment and sensitivity.

You may be thinking, "I couldn't be that active. I'm not an aggressive person." If so, experiment with the more active recommendations and see if you experience success. If you're hesitant, try some of the tactics you rated as a 4 or 5. They represent a safer place to start. Throughout this chapter you'll learn concrete tips for initiating an active search.

Your search will require the spectrum of active and passive search techniques. For example, you might submit your resume to a local employer you found on Craigslist (passive). When you don't hear back within ten days you call the company's hiring manager to make certain they received your resume (active).

Seven Stages of Getting a Job

Going from graduate school to business is a process. It will take time. There are many ways to demarcate the stages of this process. See if this seven step model is helpful.

1. **Deciding on Business.** Switching from academics to business is a major career change that often causes a significant adjustment to your personal identity.

2. **Selecting a Career Strategy.** Given the scope of the business world, you must decide where and how you want to enter this new realm. You can begin by narrowing your focus to a few industries and occupational career paths that appeal to you.

3. **Assembling Your Resources.** The job-search journey will require several important tools, including: defining your brand, creating your network, developing your elevator pitch, and writing your resume.

4. **Refining Your Skills.** Keep utilizing the tools and resources you've developed. Work on expanding your network. Ask about job leads and the names of people who might know of openings.

5. **Conducting the Search.** Now is the time to get into the marketplace and actively pursue job interviews.

6. **Landing the Offer.** In the interview process, you must distinguish yourself from other people who are seeking the same job.

7. **Getting the Best Job.** After your diligent search, it's tempting to say "Yes" to the first offer. Of course you'll look at the salary and benefits, but remember you want a job that also provides learning and career opportunities.

You've completed the first four steps. Now it's time to find job listings and schedule interviews. *Where* do you start?

Government Sites

"Fish where the fish are" is practical wisdom when it comes to sales. It also applies to fishing for jobs. Doesn't it make sense to check out the country's biggest employer, government agencies? Federal, state, and local governments employ huge numbers of people, and they're always hiring. Job security and benefits have traditionally been better in government jobs than in private organizations.

The starting jobs many not sound very alluring, but that's the price of admission. Once you're working inside the federal, state, or local governments, it's much easier to advance, and to move between departments and agencies, within each system. This is the ideal setting to use your good–better–best career strategy.

In the past, there was a central registry and a civil service exam for all U.S. government jobs. While it's not so simple anymore, there is an outstanding central website (usajobs.gov) that serves as a gateway to jobs at all federal agencies. Be sure to open the "Info Center" tab, which gives a great overview of how to apply. The description of resume tips is a must. It's applicable to government and non-government jobs. Your local and state governments will also have informative websites. Look for government recruiters at university job fairs.

For grad students who love to teach, public education could be an ideal career. Hiring is done by local school districts, so you'll need to search their websites. Smaller university towns are a very difficult place to get a teaching position, especially if the university has a school of education. While it's worth trying the local district, you should plan on casting a wider geographic net.

Small Business

Talk about a secret fishing hole, this is it. Small businesses, ones that employ fewer than 500 people (frequently many fewer) are the greatest job generators in the U.S. economy. Small doesn't mean the mom-and-pop retail store. It refers to companies located in the nondescript building complexes inelegantly called "industrial parks." Undistinguished as the exterior structures may look, you'll be amazed by the sophisticated activities that go on inside. Drive around a few of these complexes, and scope out the different companies that call this home. A small company could be a great place to start your career.

Despite the fact that small businesses are among the best places to find a starting job, career centers and guidebooks neglect to tout their virtues. Instead, their suggestions focus on large corporations with highly recognizable names and brand logos. While there's a cachet to dropping Fortune 500 corporate names, in reality most graduates will begin with a small company.

Small businesses have many benefits. You can find them in your own backyard. Since many members in your network live in this vicinity, it's highly likely they know people who work in, or even own, these businesses. Because they're in your neighborhood, it's easier to call and set up an informational interview with key managers. Better yet, walk in and try to introduce yourself to one of the managers. Try this in the middle of the week, rather than on Mondays or Fridays. Managers' workload is often heavier on these days.

One of the attributes of a *good* first job is the opportunity to learn. Although you may be starting at the bottom, in a small company you can observe and talk with the people at the top. In a small business you'll have direct contact with people in all of the company's departments and functional areas. You'll probably have lunch with them. You'll also learn about the industry, the company, and its primary customers and suppliers.

Don't be fooled by size. Many of these companies conduct business all over the world, and have very advanced business practices. They may outsource much of their production, or work with partner companies around the globe. Often they use very advanced technologies.

Small businesses are started by entrepreneurs who have found a unique niche in the market, or who have developed an innovative product. These companies go through a life cycle that's comparable to the human stages of childhood, adolescence, and adulthood. After becoming established as a startup company, successful firms experience a state of expansive growth, and then move into a slower-growth maturity. Being hired during the expansion phase, and participating in the wild ride, can be exhilarating. Larger companies often purchase or acquire these small firms that have a potential for even greater growth. Not all startups are successful, and this can make the ride risky.

Small businesses have to be highly adaptable to changing market conditions. You'll observe and participate in these sudden changes in strategy and direction. These businesses can be a great introduction to the competition inherent in free enterprise. If you select a company that is growing, there will be opportunities to assume significant responsibilities and advance your career.

Small companies are often the birthplace of innovation. For example, small businesses are among the most innovative companies in the field of energy conservation, including solar and battery technology. Working in a company that's breaking new ground generates a special excitement and commitment among employees. Co-workers have strong feelings of camaraderie.

Many people are reluctant to go into business because they feel they'll become invisible. Small companies offer a solution. In a small firm, "team effort" takes on a very real meaning. You know everyone from the bottom to the top. Work associates can easily become friends in a small company. You celebrate victories together and commiserate over setbacks. You'll feel completely involved when the company succeeds, because you'll know you were part of the team effort.

Nonprofits

Service organizations may have an international scope (e.g., Red Cross) or be very narrowly focused (local watercolor society). Some nonprofits closely parallel the operations of comparable for-profit organizations. For example, nonprofit credit unions provide banking services, and some hospitals are nonprofit while others are profit based. A nonprofit organization could be a natural fit for grad students with a community service orientation.

Although they're not driven by the bottom line of profit, all nonprofits are basically businesses. They have a budget, "customers," and an ongoing need for income. They may generate money through donations, grants, educational programs, or services. This can also be a great crucible in which to learn about business.

Even large nonprofits are closely tied to their immediate geographic community, so they tend to post jobs on websites and newspapers that service the local community. You may be able to get a list of nonprofit organizations from the local Chamber of Commerce (also a nonprofit organization).

There is one nonprofit where you have a distinct advantage—your university. In a sense you are an insider—you know the organization. Make it a point to regularly check the university's list of job openings. Many people build long-term careers within one school. Others use a university job as a platform to move to another school, or to a career in a for-profit business. Use your connections within the university to gain inside knowledge of the latest openings.

Focused Job Listings

Local newspapers, the publications of professional associations, and industry-specific newsletters (and their web sites) can be a source for legitimate job listings. Professional and industry organizations usually focus on positions for more experienced workers. They may require you to become a member to gain access to their listings. If you're certain of the industry, or type of work you want, joining may be a worthwhile investment. Someone in your network may be willing to scan these members-only websites on your behalf.

Online Postings and Scams

Swindlers, sharks, con artists and thieves have fashioned some very clever ways to take advantage of people looking for jobs. They know that when someone is desperate, they'll often be more willing to grasp at any straw. Since con artists frequently change their company name, email address, and website design, you can find a list of current scams and cons at JobsA2B.com. Here are some to avoid.

Be wary of jobs that claim you can work from home and make a good income (e.g., in one version you only have to conduct surveys). You may be "interviewed and hired" by phone and then told you'll need to purchase necessary materials, training, or equipment to begin working. Once you send your check (please don't give them your credit card information) you'll never hear from them again. Expect messages to be returned as undeliverable. In another version, they send you checks or money orders, and you're asked to simultaneously wire money to alleged vendors and suppliers. In a few days, your existing accounts are wiped out because they sent you a fraudulent check to deposit.

Searching Major Job Websites

Careerbuilder.com, monster.com, yahoohotjobs.com, collegegrad.com, and craigslist.org are large job sites where legitimate employers list openings. These major job sites have many listings and are widely used by job seekers. If you're hunting a starting job that doesn't require specialized skills or extensive work experience, you'll face stiff competition. After investing the time to sort through hundreds of job listings, and separating the bogus from those that are real, you'll still have a very low response rate to your application or resume.

If you can afford the time, it's worth monitoring these sites. Look for local companies you can personally contact and research. Your chances also improve if you identify a specific employment niche that matches your skills, and then concentrate on searching only in that domain.

While all these major web sites attempt to block and eliminate sham ads, they don't catch them all. The scammers are nefarious, and despite security measures, they occasionally infiltrate these generally reputable sites. In some cases, you're required to pay for services before you can gain access to thousands of supposed listings.

Be alert for the bait-and-switch technique. The appearance of the job listing may be very credible (including corporate logos and false websites). They'll call shortly after you submit your resume, and regretfully inform you the job was filled yesterday. Then they'll say you can get an even better job if you'll pay for their job search services. Be deeply suspicious of anyone, especially online, who promises to find you a job for a fee.

Unfortunately, "starter job" is not a job title. Organizations use very different terms to describe the starter positions you are hunting. Clearly, you're unlikely to qualify for jobs with titles that include words such as Senior, Manager, or Supervisor. It's only by reading the details that you can determine whether the job fits your profile. Words like assistant, management trainee, and associate (a synonym for employee) usually designate beginning jobs. You can also use the salary as a clue, since starting jobs are at the lower end of the pay scale.

As you read the details, focus on skill and experience requirements. Don't exclude yourself from jobs requiring two or three years of experience. If the work is directly related to your discipline, you can convincingly present your graduate school experience as fulfilling this requirement.

You may want to look at a job board's entire postings for a certain geographic area, say within 25 miles of your home. You'll have to scan all the listings to eliminate the ones that don't fit your profile. As you read these descriptions, make a list of common key words. The cover letter and resume you send a company should include buzz words and other key words from the job description. This process of sorting through job postings is time consuming and usually has a low likelihood of success.

If you're looking for a local full- or part-time job to cover expenses, try snagajob.com. Most of their listings are for hourly jobs in retail and franchise businesses. Although the franchises claim to provide a long-term career track, you'll probably only want to use these jobs as an interim position. It can be a ground level way to learn about business, and it could be a plus on your resume.

Career Centers

Your university career center may have an online resource for job listings. Many of the listings will be from national and global firms, but others will target students at your university. Many of these organizations are specifically looking to fill entry-level positions. This is also a good place for local part-time jobs and internship listings.

You may have a career fair on campus. These events occur early in the fall and spring semesters, and provide students with direct access to organizations recruiting new hires. The representatives will be happy to describe their company and the kind of job openings that are available. It's best to go early. The representatives won't be overwhelmed, and you'll have a better chance to discuss possible jobs. These recruiters don't conduct formal interviews at the fair. Make sure to bring business cards and copies of your resume.

University career centers also provide facilities for on-campus interviews. Typically, organizations who have either participated in a job fair or who have posted a job online will contact candidates and interview them on campus.

Your local or regional government may also have a career center that provides useful services. Some centers are restricted to people who receive unemployment benefits, while other centers will provide services to any resident. Their job listings are typically for manual labor or hourly positions.

Your Network

Remember death, taxes, and networking? Once again, the people you know should be directly involved in your search process. At the minimum, you should tell them you're looking for a starting job and ask them to stay alert for any openings they come across. As the scope of your search narrows, you'll be able to network more closely with individuals that have connections to companies and industries that interest you. Their knowledge of the company and people who work on the inside could be especially useful as you prepare for an interview. Reach out to your network for any assistance they can provide.

It's a Job

Searching for a job—is a job. It requires many hours of work, and it will be burdensome at times. You'll have to clear space on your computer and bookshelves for all the materials you'll gather. The next chapter describes the research process. You'll need to develop a system for storing and retrieving the information you uncover.

If the financial wolf is at your door, or worse yet, inside your home, you'll be highly motivated to step up your job search. Without a pressing need, it's easy to procrastinate and get sidelined by distractions. Just as an exercise buddy can get you to the gym on days you'd rather stay home, members of your S&A group can serve as an inspiration. Chapter 24 provides detailed advice on how to structure your days and weeks to most effectively look for a job.

20

Research and Informational Interviews

Decathlon athletes are highly admired because they compete in ten different track and field events. Most of these athletes excel in one or two events, and are average or below average in the others. As you've been reading about the job search process, you may have wondered: when will there be something I'm good at? Here it is—research. You're highly skilled at gathering reference material, reading and assimilating information, extracting the key points, and sharing what you've found. There's an abundance of job-search sources to research, and they're readily available.

One of the great fringe benefits of being a grad student is having access to your university's career center. Although these centers are used almost exclusively by undergraduates, grad students are always welcome. Not only will your current school have a center, your undergrad school probably has one. too. Recently, universities have been making a greater effort to encourage alumni to use their career centers. Go online to discover which services they offer, such as career counseling, seminars, information guides to the job search process, job listings, and ways to network with alumni.

Before the Job Interview

The concepts of industries and careers were introduced in Chapter 8, and some of that information will be repeated here in the context of actually conducting research on these two topics. In the same way, informational interviews have been introduced in several places, and that is another type of research.

This chapter necessarily repeats some information as it details exactly how these interviews should be arranged and conducted.

A wide-mouthed funnel, which narrows to a small spout, is used as a metaphor for the writing structure of a research report. This same broad-to-narrow model applies to researching jobs. The site WETFEET.COM provides a range of job search information. The careers and industries tab is a good starting point.

Industries

The web is a cornucopia of information about every industry. Insert the word "industry" after your favorites and start exploring. The first sites belong to commercial organizations that sell training programs or access to job listings (if you search under the industry name and "jobs" you'll be inundated with commercial sites). These are followed by noncommercial sites that contain a wealth of information. Professional associations, government agencies, independent research organizations, and journalists' articles also provide a good foundation for understanding each industry.

Industry-based organizations have strong vested interests and will put a positive patina on even the worst situations. Reviews and assessments in the general business media, as well as business analysts, provide a more realistic perspective. If you or someone in your network has connections to a stock brokerage house, or mutual fund firm, it could be useful to learn how their technical specialists evaluate the industry. Hoovers.com has a comprehensive survey of industries and sub-sectors.

As you gain an understanding of the sub-sectors within an industry, you'll begin to develop a sense of areas that fit your profile. Which of your skills fit best with the industry, and which industry meshes with your values and interests? What is the general level of compensation? What are the dominant companies? Are they centered in a geographic area? Which jobs and careers seem to be most highly valued in the industry? What is the image of the industry among business people and with the general public? Which sub-sectors have the best future growth opportunities?

Many industries are cyclical. One that is down today could be rising in six months. Conversely, the one that appears to be riding high may be on the verge of a collapse. Learn about the industry's historic economic cycle. Is it growing, declining or stable? When an industry or company is referred to as "mature," this means it's reached its full growth potential. Independent analysts and journalists will give you the most accurate estimate of an industry's economic trends, and the implications this data will have on your career.

Career Functions

An excellent source of career information is the *Occupational Outlook Handbook* published by the Bureau of Labor Statistics (bls.gov/oco/). Your career center probably has a hardcopy.

Your personal knowledge, abilities, skills, interests, and personality are closely associated with the kinds of activities you enjoy. Naturally, they are closely linked to the career function in which you'll find the best fit. Just as industries have sub-sectors, career fields have sub-specialties. People who work in human resources may be generalists, or specialists in areas such as benefits, compensation, diversity, education, employment, and law. Understanding these sub-specialties may help you clarify the type of job you want.

Plan an informational interview with at least five people in any field that interests you. Everyone has their unique subjective perspective, but certain constants will emerge as you talk with more people. Most people take pride in the work they do, and they like to advise people just beginning their careers. Unless they're swamped with work, most people will be more than happy to talk on the phone or in person for an informational interview.

If you are actively pursuing a job, you can make cold calls to people with local companies. Make it clear this is an information-only interview. If you're hesitant about making a cold call, then treat this exercise as a research or writing project. When you call, explain that you're interviewing people as part of a research study for other grad students—your S&A team.

Companies

Hoovers.com has a comprehensive survey of companies. After you create a list of desirable firms, visit each company's website. General business publications, industry publications and websites may be useful sources of information. You can often find news stories about even the smallest company. You'll be able to get answers to these basic questions:

Where is the company headquarters located?
Do they have other major locations?
Who is the CEO or president?
Who is responsible for the department where you'd work?
Have senior executives recently joined or departed the company?
What are the major product lines and services?
Have they recently launched a new product or service (or, are they about to)?
What market segments do they serve?
Who are their prime customers?

Who are their prime competitors?

What was their financial performance in the past quarter, year, 5 years?

What are the performance estimates for the next: quarter, year, 5 years?

What is their current business strategy?

Are they a takeover candidate, or are they considering an acquisition?

Use your research to conduct your own SWOT analysis of the company.

Every company has a few disgruntled employees. Some of them blog or create a forum for likeminded people. These sources may give you more information than you want, but they may also raise a few questions you'll want to diplomatically address in an informational interview.

Another great way to learn about companies is by attending on-campus presentations by representatives of the company. Some career centers organize these company profile events. Most business schools have a career center that is dedicated to their MBA students. Although they can't give you career advice, they should be willing to tell you how you can learn about business presentations on campus. Every semester, the business school sponsors lectures and presentations. Unless the room is filled to capacity, you'll be welcome. You may also be able to introduce yourself to people before and after the event.

The Yellow Pages, and other business directories, are the best source of contact information for local companies. Small companies are an excellent way to begin a career, because you get a comprehensive picture of the overall operation. In large corporations you're usually in a very narrow niche, in one small location of a global enterprise.

Job Search Process

While you're researching industries and careers, you'll encounter tips and insights into the job search process. This information may be specific to a particular type of job or it may be more general. JobsA2B.com provides a list of books and websites that can provide more detailed information about the search process. One of the best books for practical tips is *The College Grad Job Hunter.* Although it is geared to people just completing an undergraduate degree, the many examples are illuminating and you can easily make the extrapolation to your situation. Many of the suggestions can be applied to your own resume, cover letters, network, and interviews. Since the rituals of business are different from those of academia, you should delve into descriptions of business etiquette and accepted manners of the job search process. Finally, remember the usajobs.gov website for job search advice.

If you uncover a news release or announcement that a member of your network received a promotion or recognition for an achievement, send them a personalized congratulatory message.

Remain on the alert for information about short courses that would improve your business skills. Courses and programs sponsored by government agencies and community colleges are usually free, or relatively low-cost.

Don't Research

A few employers may ask you to take a personality test as part of the hiring process. These are rarely part of an initial interview, but could be part of a call-back process. Some people get unnecessarily worried about these tests, and want to learn the best way to answer each question. If you want to learn a little about the structure and purpose of the test, that's fine, but *don't* get stressed about how to answer the questions.

The primary use of these screening tests is to identify extreme personalities. They want to catch people who might create serious problems. Answer the questions truthfully, and you'll have nothing to worry about. Don't try to memorize answers (usually the number of questions will exceed your memory).

There are other tests to assess your interests and personal strengths. These are used as a basis for predicting whether you'll fit into a particular type of work. You probably have the maturity and good sense to apply only for positions that fit your personal profile, but perhaps your self-assessment is wrong. If the company can determine that you're a mismatch for its needs, then you want to find out. You don't want to get trapped in a job you'd hate.

Storage and Sharing

You're going to compile a great deal of information and you'll need a system to store and retrieve it. Some of the information will be electronically based and some will be hardcopy. You'll probably use both your computer and a physical filing system. When you begin mailing resumes and responding to interview invitations, you'll also need an organized system to keep track of the nature and date of your contacts.

One of the chief activities of a Search and Assist group is to share research. Get in the habit of providing an executive summary and a guide to action steps. If you're writing a blog, you might want to post some of the information, or make it available through an online forum.

For a Job Interview

When you're invited for an interview, you'll want detailed information about the company. Large corporations publish an annual report. Try and read the most recent version. If you can't get it online, try writing the company. Pay particular attention to the strategy statement. See if you can determine the link between the work you might be doing and the company's stated strategy. You might want to explore this topic with the interviewer when you're asked if you have any questions. Begin by asking if the company is still pursuing this strategy, and how it's progressing. Ask how the activities of your potential department are linked to supporting the strategic goals.

Become familiar with the names of the company's senior leaders. Try to learn the company's organizational structure, and identify the C-level executive responsible for your department. Many departments report to one senior person. You'll want to know where your department ranks on this executive's list of priorities.

You'll need to do even more research when you're invited back for a second interview. You may only know the name of the department, and not the name of your supervisor. You may be able to deduce it from your research, or through a contact in your network.

When the interviewer first tells you the supervisor's name, ask them to repeat the name for you. With novel names you may need to clarify the pronunciation ("Can you help me with the pronunciation of his name?"). Practice it several times with the interviewer to avoid future mispronunciations. You want to be well prepared when you actually meet the individual.

During the second interview, you'll most likely learn about the salary and benefits of the job. In anticipation of this discussion, you might visit your career center for a directory of the average salary received for comparable jobs in your region.

Informational Interviews

Informational interviews are conducted to gather information, not to get a job. These formal discussions are scheduled in advance. Since the other person is doing you a favor, be sensitive to their time constraints and schedule. Make the interview at a time and place that's convenient for them. The typical interview will be 15–60 minutes long and can be on the telephone or in person. A face-to-face meeting at the individual's workplace is ideal. You'll get to see inside the facility, and possibly meet some of the other employees.

Informational interviews are *not* job interviews. This golden rule needs to be restated. Your interview can backfire if you tell someone you're only interested in information, and then make a pitch for a job. They'll get angry and spread the word. This bad publicity could infect your network. The technique has been tried many times before. So remember: don't ask, don't drop hints, or even innuendos, and don't mention anything about a job in your thank-you note.

Let the other person take any initiative. They know you're in the job market. If they notice something about you that indicates you'd make a good hire, they'll draw this conclusion on their own. The rules change if they volunteer information about possible openings, or ask if you'd consider a job with the firm. If—and only if—they take the lead, should you express your interest in a position.

Make it clear when you request the interview that it is for information only. Tell them the specific topics you want to discuss. Offer to send a list of the basic questions (do not include your resume unless it's requested). When you write to confirm the time of your appointment, reiterate the informational nature of the interview. At the beginning of the meeting, thank the person for agreeing to this "information-only interview."

You'll probably start with small talk as you get acquainted. Before you begin your questioning, ask if you can take some notes. The person shouldn't mind. Your note-taking affirms the importance of the information they're sharing. It also provides a discrete way to read rather than memorize your key questions.

There's no prescribed order for your questions. You might begin by asking their reasons for choosing this industry. They'll relax as you begin the conversation with such general inquiries as:

- How did you get started in this industry (name their industry)?
- What factors influenced your decision to work in this industry?
- Have you worked for other companies in this industry?
- Why did you select this company?

After you've established a comfort level with one another, you can get to more substantive questions. If you are interested in learning about their industry, you might adapt some of the following questions:

- What parts of the industry have the greatest potential for growth?
- Are there any parts of the industry that have reached a plateau?
- What kind of work experience best prepares people for this industry?
- What kind of education is most helpful for working in this industry?
- What kinds of people succeed in this industry?

- How should a beginner get started in this industry?
- What do you see as the key to success in this industry?
- What do you wish you had known before you got into this business?
- In this industry, are career advancement opportunities more accessible for people in one department over another?
- Which companies will be able to take advantage of growth opportunities?

Your goal is to get information, so don't make references to yourself and your qualifications unless you're asked.

Another major topic for an informational interview is to learn about careers in their field (e.g., marketing, human resources, project management, manufacturing, etc.). Since this could be a lengthy conversation, you may want to limit the interview to either the topic of their industry or their work. Don't overstay your welcome. Prioritize your questions for a 15, 30, or 60-minute interview.

You can begin by slightly modifying a few of the questions you used to initiate the interview on industries.

- Have you always worked in this area (name the work area)?
- How did you begin your business career?
- What is your educational background?
- What other fields did you try?

Now you can move the focus to the topic of careers.

- What do you enjoy most about your work?
- What kinds of people are best suited for this type of work?
- What kind of education will best prepare someone for this field?
- What kind of work experience best prepares people for this type of work?
- What do you see as the keys to success in this field?
- What do you wish you had known before you got into this field?
- How should a beginner get started in this field?
- If you were starting your career over again, what would you do differently?
- Did you make any blunders in your career? What lessons did you learn?
- Do people in this field move into upper management?

These model questions are only meant to lay the foundation. Select the questions that best reflect the areas of greatest interest to you, and then translate them into your own words and phrases. Conclude the interview with an open ended question such as:

- Do you have any general advice for someone just beginning a career?
- Are there any other questions I should have asked you?

Finally, you should ask permission to re-contact them if you have any further questions. You might use wording such as: "If I think of any questions, would you mind if I sent you an email?" When you get a job interview with another company, you may want to ask for their advice.

Just as with a job interview, send a brief email or thank-you note within 24–36 hours of the interview. It should highlight one key idea you gained from the discussion. Some people take a card and envelope with them, so they can write a note immediately after the interview. You should also rewrite and condense your interview notes while the event is still fresh in your mind.

Informal Discussions

You can gain useful career information from almost anyone. Take advantage of opportunities to talk with all kinds of people—in restaurants, on trains, planes, at social gatherings, or in waiting areas.

Asking someone about their work is an easy ice breaker. If they seem interested in talking, inquire about their career path, what they like or dislike about their work, and what advice they have for someone just getting started. Feel free to tell them about your skills. Describe yourself in business terms. Don't share the details of your latest research project.

These unplanned discussions can sometimes end abruptly due to outside circumstances. Be prepared to quickly exchange business cards. You can contact them later if they would be a useful resource.

It can be somewhat daunting to interview a stranger for 30 minutes. If the anticipation of an informational interview feels a little overwhelming, begin by practicing your skills with a close friend or S&A partner. Rehearsing with friends and family can increase your confidence. A list of prepared questions will also help you relax.

Now you're ready to approach people whose industries and types of work are of special interest. If you are hesitant, remember—you're going through another J-Curve. After a few of these informal encounters, it will get easier. In addition to gaining valuable information, you'll also establish a new network connection. After your interview, they'll make a mental note about you and your qualifications. They might even contact you if they hear about a possible job. The relationships you establish through information gathering can become key assets to your business network.

21

Job Interviews

Ask yourself one question before you leave home: Are you pleased, or blasé about this interview? Go ahead, admit it. You're not just pleased, you're elated. After all your hard work, setbacks and disappointments, you're finally appreciated. You've earned this interview. It's okay to let your happiness show.

Meet and Greet

The interview begins the moment you leave the house, so switch into your "good manners" mode en route. The person you honk at might just be your interviewer.

If the interview takes place at the company's headquarters, the first important person you connect with will be the receptionist. This individual could have a critical voice in your fate. Since people assume you'll be more yourself in the waiting room than in the interview, the receptionist's impression can carry a great deal of weight. Don't forget she might be watching how you pace back and forth, apply lipstick six times, or make sarcastic remarks about the décor to a friend on your cell phone.

Receptionists deal with many people every day, and they have a keen sense about who might fit in with the company, and who won't. Interviewers regularly seek the receptionist's impressions about job candidates.

Many companies use the reception area to display awards, products, brochures and news clippings about the company. During your interview, you might have an opportunity to refer to an item you spotted in the waiting room.

When you are called for your appointment, make sure your smile is in place. Step forward and warmly greet the interviewer.

Handshakes are like reading a person's palm. People put great faith in the information they glean from a handshake. A firm but not bone crushing grip will help express your enthusiasm and sincerity. If you normally have a soft grip (ask your friends for an evaluation), you should practice applying a little more pressure. With practice, this handshake will feel natural. When you're ushered into the interviewer's office, smile, extend your hand and introduce yourself. Call the person by name. "Hello, I'm Gabrielle O'Toole. Are you Ms. Perez?"

As you're invited to have a seat, take a quick look around the room for mementos, awards and photos. You don't want to appear nosy, but you can comment on one item of interest. If you decide to inquire about something, first ascertain that the office belongs to the interviewer. It can start the meeting on a very embarrassing note if you "oohh and aahh" over a baby photo and then discover the baby *and* the office belong to someone else. Interviews are sometimes conducted in the most attractive office in the building. The company wants to make a good impression, too.

It's probably best to wait and get a sense of the individual and the situation before you get too personal. You don't want to look like you're trying too hard, or wasting the interviewer's time. There might be a room full of job candidates, and the interviewer may want to get right down to business. After a very brief, cordial exchange, take your seat, open your writing portfolio and prepare to begin the meeting.

Q and A

The interviewer wants to get answers to three fundamental questions:

- Who are you?
- Why should we hire you?
- What do you want from us?

Their questions can vary from the silly (What kind of animal would you like to be?) to the most detailed (When you had a summer job at Foot Locker, how many socks and T-shirts did you sell after you sold a pair of shoes?).

Your first interviewer could be from the human resources department (who is responsible for recruiting new hires). If he's favorably impressed, you'll go through a second interview with a manager from your future department. Small organizations may not have a human resource specialist, so your first interview could be with your future manager or even the CEO.

Human resource professionals are experienced and skillful. Their initial questions will be of the "tell me about yourself" variety. (Lists of common interview questions are available on the web and at JobsA2B.com.) You can begin by briefly emphasizing each of your strengths. By scripting and rehearsing your answers, you'll be able to honestly and succinctly answer the interviewer's questions.

Benefits not Attributes

Next, the interviewer may probe for details about your past work experiences, and the strengths and skills listed on your resume. Your answers should be based on a fundamental principle of sales—sell the sizzle, not the steak.

The more formal version is—sell benefits, not attributes. In sales, this means don't focus on a product's attributes, instead talk about how these qualities could benefit the customer. For example, if you're selling a laptop computer you can describe the processor specs, memory capacity, and its plug-and-play readiness. Successful salespeople quickly switch to how the attributes will benefit the customer. "Do you ever get tired waiting for a program to load, or for a website to appear? With the processor in this laptop, you'll never have to wait again."

When the interviewer asks about a specific skill, you can describe your level of knowledge and experience, and then explain how they will benefit the company. For example, after describing your knowledge of a statistical package, you can say, "I can do even the most complex multivariate analysis on the spot. You won't have to wait hours for results. And, I'll give you an honest interpretation of the implications of the results." If you indicated you are fluent in Spanish, you can describe your level of knowledge, then add, "If you normally hire a consultant to translate your documents into Spanish, I can do it and save you the expense."

If you don't know that much about the exact work, simply ask the interviewer. "If you'd be willing to tell me a little more about the work responsibilities of this job, I'd be happy to describe how I could add value to the company."

Keep your answers to no more than two minutes and preferably 30–60 seconds. A longer answer will make it more likely you might lose your train of thought, and the interviewer's attention. A better approach is to give shorter answers and ask the interviewer, "Would you like me to elaborate?" They'll have the prerogative to ask for greater detail. If they say they'd like to move on, don't be concerned. In many instances the interviewer is paying more attention to *how* you phrased your answer, than to the specifics of *what* you said. It's usually a good sign if they move on to a new question.

Difficult Questions

People are sometimes stumped by what has become the standard practice of asking about your weaknesses (many examples of these questions are available on the web). Answers such as, "I work too hard," or "Sometimes I'm just too committed to excellence," are overused and appear disingenuous. As part of your preparation, identify two or three personal weaknesses. Always describe what you are doing to overcome the weakness. Don't reveal major character flaws. Stick to traits that can be problematic in some situations.

Most graduate students suffer from a lack of work experience and the interviewer is very aware of this weakness. Why not confront the elephant in the room?

> "I haven't worked in healthcare. To make up for this deficiency I've spent time researching the industry and your company. I've also conducted 9 informational interviews. I anticipate a steep learning curve, and fortunately learning is one of my strengths."

Pause and smile at the interviewer to signal you've answered the question. This is her cue to probe further, or ask another question.

If she asks for a second weakness, be prepared.

> "I'm comfortable expressing my ideas, so I have to be careful not to be too assertive. I make it a point to let others talk before I speak. Then, I always acknowledge other people's useful comments, before offering an alternative perspective."

Conversely, "I appear shy but I'm just very thoughtful. I like to think things through before speaking. I alert people to my thoughtful style, so they're not surprised when I lay out my all my ideas."

Since you can anticipate questions about your weaknesses, you should be well prepared. Speak clearly, deliberately, and with confidence. Interviewers also ask about sensitive topics such as:

> "Are you comfortable taking orders?"
> "How do you react to criticism?"
> "Do you need praise and recognition?"
> "How do you feel about working overtime?"

It's tempting to give idealized answers (e.g., "I'm very comfortable taking orders; I love criticism and don't require constant stroking; and I'm always happy to work overtime."). Such knee-jerk answers are cloying. You're not interviewing for sainthood. These issues can be problematic for everyone. The interviewer is as interested in your honesty as in the content of your answer.

> "Like most people I don't enjoy being criticized. I always strive to do things right the first time, but naturally I'll occasionally make a mistake. I accept constructive criticism because it will enable me to learn and improve. Constructive feedback from managers and co-workers is essential for my development."

Or, "I'm prepared to work overtime, but hopefully not for months on end."

Try to link your answers back to your strengths. For example, "I don't need constant praise, but like most people I like to be recognized for major accomplishments. I'm very goal oriented. Praise helps me know that I'm succeeding."

The most difficult questions are ones that are a complete surprise. You can stall a bit by saying, "Interesting question. Can I take a moment to frame my answer?" Interviewers sometimes want to put you on the spot and watch how you handle stress. They like to observe candidates during these moments of apparent uncertainty and confusion. Don't frown, scratch your head or panic. Take your pen in hand and write a few words on your notepad. Even if you're only rewriting the question, concentrate on your writing. You'll be perceived as thoughtful and deliberate. When you have an answer, smile, look at the interviewer, and start talking.

Feel free to ask a clarifying question if you're completely stumped. "Could you please rephrase your question? I want to be sure I fully understand what you're asking." If your mind is a complete blank, ask for more time: "Would you mind if I think about your question and return to it later?" Make sure to jot down the question on your writing pad.

What kind of impression do you give the interviewer when you return to an earlier question? You validate your thoughtfulness and thoroughness. You can also try to return to any question you wish you had answered differently. This shows you're thoughtful and always want to improve your performance. A few candidates take the risky approach of deliberately giving a partial answer to a question, so they can return to it later with a more complete answer.

Behavioral Questions

Instead of asking what you *can do*, behavioral questions focus on what you've *actually done*. When you describe one of your strengths (e.g., innovative) a follow-up question from the interviewer might be: "Could you describe a specific example of when and how you found an innovative solution to a problem?" You should prepare at least two behavioral examples to illustrate each of your core strengths.

Your answer should take the form of a simple story in four chronological steps:

- The problem situation and the people involved
- How you handled the situation
- The quantitative results
- The lessons you learned

Since innovation is one your strengths, cite several well rehearsed examples.

> "Our grant money was practically gone and yet we still had several more studies to complete. A major expense was interviewing participants. I modified our interview questionnaire so we didn't have to hire professional interviewers. Our participants liked the freedom to complete their questionnaires online at their convenience. When we compared the initial online responses to our previous interview results, the responses were virtually equivalent. This solution saved almost ten thousand dollars. I learned there's always a lower-cost alternative."

Write out your behavioral answers and practice your delivery. Don't make the situation too complicated, but add a few details that will involve the listener. Don't exaggerate your contribution. You can play a feature role in the scenario, but share the credit with others (e.g., "I suggested the idea, but the team made it happen"). If you simplify the story, it will have a greater impact.

Real-World Questions

The interviewer might describe a specific challenge the company is facing. You'll be asked how you'd solve the problem. Ideally, the idea you propose might actually solve the problem, but that isn't the purpose of the question. They've undoubtedly considered many solutions. You can't be expected to have *the* answer. Instead, they want to see how you analyze the problem, what kind of solutions you generate, and how well you communicate your reasoning.

Since you have no way of knowing the questions in advance, it's impossible to have a mental file of brilliant answers. You are, however, as prepared as you could be. In grad school you've honed your analytic skills, you've practiced problem solving, and you've learned how to logically advance and defend an idea.

As the interviewer describes the situation, you can ask additional probing questions and jot down notes. Be sure to inquire about the company's current way of dealing with the problem, as well as other solutions they've tried or considered. By asking these questions you're indicating your approach to problems. Begin your answer by summarizing the situation and defining the problem. Next, describe what has been tried and propose your own solutions. Present the advantages and disadvantages of your recommendations. You don't have to endorse one solution, unless the interviewer pointedly asks which one you favor. You might conclude with a statement such as, "I'd also share my ideas with my manager, or my team, and ask for their perspectives about how to proceed."

Why Do You Want to Work Here?

Grad students must be prepared for this question. Interviewers ask it in many forms, and your responses are especially critical. This is your opportunity to erase any doubts they might have about your commitment to business. Every candidate claims to really want the job, so your answer must emphatically communicate a sincere desire to get *this* job. Don't sound desperate: "I've been eating rice for months. Finally I won't have to live in my car."

Your research about the firm and the industry can supply the basis of your answer. If the company is doing well, you want to help it grow. If it's in a slump, you want to help turn it around. Explain why you believe this company has a great future. You can cite: the leadership, the new strategic direction, or the latest products. Are you attracted to the company's culture? Are you excited about the work you would be doing and the people you'd work with? You can identify two or three key factors in advance and be ready to explain why they make you want to work for this company. Show your enthusiasm.

Your answer doesn't have to be long, but must come from your heart. The fact that you can cite specific details about the company shows your degree of interest. Conclude your remarks by linking your enthusiasm to your key strengths and by explicitly stating: "I sincerely hope to have the opportunity to become part of this organization.

Questions to Ask

Most interviewers will give you an opportunity to ask questions. In the best of circumstances, this will occur early in the interview. This will enable you to tie your future answers to the information you acquire from the interviewer. Bring a list of questions such as:

> Could you tell me more about the exact work I might be doing?
> How many people are on the team, and what are their backgrounds?
> Is this a new position? If so, why was it created?
> Is the last person still with the firm, or did they move on? (Note: if the person is still at the firm, you might talk to them after you have the job. Explain to the interviewer that such a discussion might help you get up to speed.)
> What are the keys to success in this job?
> What are the most frequent mistakes people make in this job?
> What is the expected career track for someone in this position?
> Do you have any suggestions for the person fortunate enough to be hired?

Notice, you aren't asking about salary and benefits. Wait until they raise the topic.

For a starting position, most companies have budgeted a specific salary, so there won't be much room to negotiate. You may be given a starting salary range (e.g., between $45,000 and $52,000). Smile at the information, and immediately ask about the factors that move people to the top of the range. This information will enable you to prepare your case for why you deserve to be hired at a higher salary. Or, you might be told that based on your performance you could be eligible for an X percent raise in three or six months. Again, find out the standards by which your performance will be judged. You may be able to negotiate the percent increase be moved upward (e.g., from 5% to 10%).

Concluding the Interview

Wait for the interviewer to signal the end of the discussion. The interviewer will often stand up and thank you for coming, and will discuss next steps. If next steps aren't mentioned, feel free to inquire when you'll hear from the interviewer.

Express your gratitude for the meeting and the opportunity to learn more about the company. Then, praise the interviewer for how s/he handled the session. Support your general praise for the interviewer by mentioning at least one specific thing they said or did.

> "You really made me feel comfortable. For example, when you asked about my customer service experience, you told me it was okay to take a minute and collect my thoughts. You showed a sensitivity that is rare and much appreciated. Thank you."

Or, "I liked how you asked for details about the nature of the teamwork in my research group. This is also my style. I want to make sure I understand what people mean when they communicate."

Interviewers expect the candidate to say thank you; however, they'll be surprised and impressed when you offer feedback. The feedback becomes more unique when you bolster your praise with a behavioral example from the interview. This final demonstration of your sensitivity and maturity will confirm that you're the person for the job.

22

Sweating the Details

How many graduate students eagerly anticipate the day they must go before a committee for an all-important oral exam? The answer is almost *zero*. No one likes being scrutinized, and the experience becomes especially stressful when your entire future depends on the verdict. In academics you won't be rejected because you wore the wrong shoes to your oral exam. In a job interview you might be.

During the job search process, the smallest misstep can cost you a job. A typo on an email, arriving late for an appointment, your cell phone ringing in the middle of an interview – these are absolute DON'Ts. One of these errors won't automatically spell doom. Cumulatively, they could tip the scales in favor of your competitor. You can improve your chances of getting a job by refining the tiny details that might make all the difference.

Interviewers need to be on the alert for any clue that might raise a red flag. There's too much at stake for them and their company. They'll pay attention to both your personal style as well as to the substance of your answers. Some interviewers give special credence to gestures and unguarded actions. They believe little things can reveal significant positives *and* negatives.

You can use this career change as an opportunity to make a few adjustments to your personal identity. You may have already suspected that certain aspects of your student life should be left behind. Now is the time to come into your own as a mature professional.

Who Are You?

You're entering a new world of people who know very little about you. You have the luxury of introducing yourself with any name you choose. Chapter 13 addressed the subject of "branding." Your name is a crucial part of your brand identity. Perhaps you've always been known by a nickname (which you never liked). Now's the time to switch. A redhead named Rusty went back to his full name, Russell. And Shug (for sugar) wanted to be less sweet and more serious, so he reverted to Justin.

Your friends may question and even tease you about your name, but they'll get used to it. A first step might be printing your business cards. Every time you look at the card, your name will reaffirm the new you and your new career.

Your Electronic Identity

Now is the time to "graduate" into the business world. Upgrade your public image by reevaluating the photos and descriptions you've posted online. You don't want your online identity to be inconsistent with the image of maturity and responsibility you're trying to convey. Your private life is yours alone, so keep it to yourself. Expect interested employers to search every social network site. Sweep the web and delete any information that makes you appear frivolous or tarnishes your image of trustworthiness and stability. You're applying for a job, not for a match on soulmate.com.

It's easy to obtain a free email address to use for business-related messages. Avoid clever or suggestive words in your address, and stick to nondescript variations of your name. You'll be able to substitute a *.com* or *.net* for a . *edu*, which suggests you're still in school.

Phone messages that seem funny to fellow students may not be as humorous to potential employers. Keep to the basics. Say, "Thank you for the call. Please leave your name and number." You never know when an interviewer might call. Always practice good phone manners. Answer with a simple "Hello" (i.e. not "Yeah," or "Speak")

Stick to the facts when you leave a message. When you say your name and number, speak slowly. There's a good chance the person is picking up 20 messages in the cacophony of an airport. Say your name and number twice, and the second time don't simply list the numbers, "...7, 0, 2, 2." Find a way to make them distinctive, "That's 70, 22."

Your Written Identity

The job search process has a formal ritual which applies to everything you write. Be extremely careful when transmitting any written message.

Treat business emails as if they were handwritten letters. Unless a message requires your immediate response, write a first draft, leave it for a couple of hours and then recheck for spelling errors, sentence structure and content.

Your Appearance

In the first 15 seconds of an interview, your appearance could have as much effect as your subsequent words. It's ironic that if you're perfectly dressed, the interviewer might not even notice. If your attire is inappropriate, however, they'll give you the once-over immediately. You want to communicate that you mean business, so reinforce that sentiment with your clothing. This doesn't mean you should dress for a funeral. Your outfit should, however, be discreet and lean toward the conservative. If you think the company may have a very relaxed dress code, contact the interviewer prior to the meeting and ascertain the appropriate style of dress.

You'll need a suit or a business outfit. It's not imperative to wear a designer label, but your clothing must fit and be unobtrusive. Don't wear a white suit (even in the summer). Choose dark blue or black. The suit should be plain without patterns or stripes. Wear a white blouse or shirt. Choose simple leather shoes in blue or black for women, and black for men. If you have doubts about what is appropriate, go to a good clothing store and ask for recommendations. There are many discount clothing stores that carry business attire. You may find very inexpensive designer labels and other bargains at vintage or used clothing stores.

Yes, your "interview" outfit should be on the boring side. For a job interview, your individuality is expressed through your talent, skill, and business savvy. In addition to wearing an understated suit, your accessories (as well as your makeup and hairstyle) should be as simple as possible. Loud neckties, gaudy jewelry, and iridescent scarves can detract from your business demeanor.

Make sure your clothing fits. Check that your hemline and pant cuffs are even. Since neckties are rarely worn, men sometimes have difficulty adjusting to the feel of a buttoned shirt collar. They mistakenly try to avoid the problem by purchasing a shirt that is too large. The salesperson will measure your neck. Follow their recommendation. Wear the shirt at home for several hours to become accustomed to the feeling of fabric touching your neck. You don't want to pull at your collar during the interview. If you don't know how to tie a neck-tie, a salesperson will show you how. They'll also demonstrate the proper way to remove the tie without untying it, so you can use it again.

The perfect accessory to your business attire is a portfolio with a writing tablet inside. Instead of stuffing your resume, notepad and other papers into your purse or backpack, you might want to purchase an inexpensive portfolio or small briefcase. Many discount stores carry portfolios (in materials that look exactly like leather) at very reasonable prices. If the price is still too high, you might borrow a portfolio from a member of your S&A group. Another important DON'T in an interview is fumbling through your briefcase for a paper covered with post-it notes. If you're going to carry a briefcase or portfolio, make sure you've organized the contents well in advance of your interview. You should be able to reach in and grab Exhibit A, or a resume.

Interviewers' number-one complaint about clothing is that people dress too casually. It's hard to believe, but some aspiring employees actually show up in flip flops or athletic shoes. Young women mistakenly dress as though they're going clubbing. Too much perfume or aftershave can be offensive and might cost you the job. Make sure you're well scrubbed, and that your hair is neatly combed. Tastes are changing in body art (a term invented by the tattoo industry), but most employers prefer that you display your art on the weekend.

Your Manners

The acronym IPO stands for Initial Public Offering. (It describes a privately owned company that "goes public" by selling shares in the firm.) *Going public* is how you should approach the day of your job interview. The moment you go out your door, anyone and everyone you encounter might have a connection to your prospective company. Suffice it to say, *be on your best behavior.*

If you enter a doorway at the same time as someone else, always defer to the other person. One applicant, who was running a little late, unknowingly stepped in front of a person who turned out to be the interviewer. You aren't even safe in the company bathroom. An overly fastidious candidate began floss-ing his teeth in the men's room, much to the shock of another man washing his hands (who, of course, turned out to be the interviewer).

A day for two before the interview, rehearse your route to the site. Map out the journey on a business day, so you can measure the traffic. Always plan to arrive 15 to 30 minutes early. Rather than sitting around the reception area, find a quiet place to relax and get focused. Don't enter the building more than ten minutes before the appointed time. Turn off your telephone and any electronic device that might ring, beep, vibrate or play a loud tune.

Older generations tend to criticize young people for having a sense of entitlement. The implication is that Generation Y feels they deserve elevated positions and perks without paying their dues. In most cases, this is a completely unfounded stereotype. You need to be aware of these preconceptions so that you won't do anything to reinforce this bias. How would you behave the first time you meet your future in-laws? That's the way to act on a job interview. Be extremely polite, and always express your gratitude. If you have a special request, begin by asking permission: "Would you mind if I briefly describe my interpersonal skills?"

There are endless horror stories about tiny errors sabotaging an entire interview. You don't want to become a statistic. Everything you do and say can and *might* be held against you when you're on a job interview.

Practice

Just as you should rehearse your route to the interview site, you should go over your answers and your delivery.

Although practice won't make you perfect, it will make you more confident. As you repeat your answers, you'll become more relaxed. Your natural enthusiasm will shine through your words and facial expressions. Ironically, repetition actually enables you to be more spontaneous. Knowing exactly what you want to say, and how you want to say it, will allow the real you to shine through. You won't be able to anticipate all the questions. Even so, you'll find ways to weave in the myriad of answers you've been practicing.

23

Working Your Plan

Is there anything you know you should do, but you're not doing? How about: eat healthy foods, exercise regularly, get an annual health checkup, and spend time with your family. There's often an inconsistency between our values and what we do. This disjuncture is called the "knowing/doing gap." Now that you know how to get a business job, you need to do it. Sometimes that's easier said than done.

From the starting point of your journey, the uphill climb can look long and difficult. Although challenging, it's nothing compared to the sacrifices you were making to become a professor. You were willing to commit yourself to years of grad school. Locating a job in business won't require years, but it will require a daily commitment to action.

Taking the first steps from Stage 1 to Stage 2 of a major change can seem impossibly difficult for some people. They feel like an outsider, as though they don't have the qualifications to ask for a job in business. They may feel "less than," or not good enough to get a job. These self-doubts create a condition known as concrete feet. Your feet feel so heavy, you can't even lift them to take the first steps. These feelings are normal, and fortunately there is a cure.

Small Goals

Remember the earlier recommendation to take baby steps and use ground level language? The longest journey does begin with a single step, and it continues with many more small steps. Be very specific about setting goals for this week, this day, this morning, and possibly even the next hour. The concept of SMART goals is very popular in business. This acronym is a way of remembering that goals should be: Specific, Measurable, Achievable, Relevant; and Timely. Research data supports this approach.

Depending on how much time you have, you might set these goals for the week: complete my elevator speech; practice it with three people; start my business network by calling 10 people, and telling them I'm looking for a job. How smart are the goals? They are fairly specific, measurable, within your capacity to achieve, relevant to your goal, and doable within a week. These are fairly modest goals for a week, but even these goals may seem unattainable.

Divide and conquer is the answer. Take each goal and separate it into parts. To construct your elevator speech, you need to use 15 minutes to write out what you have to offer people, and what assistance you're seeking. This is an even more specific goal, and it should be easier to achieve. What if your feet still feel heavy? Break down your goals even further:

"In the next 5 minutes I'm going to jot down some ideas about my elevator speech. It doesn't matter if I generate one idea or 20." Anyone can achieve this small goal. What do you think will happen if you start your list? You'll probably work past the deadline and complete a rough draft.

Make a list of goals for the week, and also for each day. Some people like to have a separate list for the A.M. and P.M. Writing out the list is a useful reminder. It feels good to cross off each accomplishment. If you are someone who doesn't use lists—start. You can start small, but start. If you don't see an improvement in your output within two weeks, return to *your* approach.

Glide Path

To achieve your SMART goals you'll need a GLIDE path. Like an airplane descending to its destination, it will help define the path to each of your goals. Define your behavioral steps in **G**round **L**evel language, specifying **I**mmediate things you can **D**o. It should be **E**asy to take these actions.

How will you practice your elevator speech? After deciding on three people, contact each of them and ask for their help. Try and set a time during the week when you can spend 20 minutes together. Although this is a simple goal, and probably won't require a written GLIDE path, it illustrates how you can tackle large and small goals.

The final **E** in *glide* is very important—make it **E**asy to take action. What would make it easy for you to practice with each person on your list? If you can't think of anything that would make it easy, try to imagine potential problems that might arise with each person. It will be easy to practice with your spouse, partner, or roommate. You might not want your partner listening while you practice with someone else. Perhaps you could meet at your office, or in a class-room on campus. Or, you might have great respect for one person, but you know he can sometimes be too opinionated. Ask him in advance to temper his criticism. When you're feeling hesitant, remove even the smallest potential obstacle. It will be easier to take the next steps.

Set a personal development goal for *how* you want to tackle your job search. You want to become a more confident speaker. You can work on this with the assistance of all three people. You may want to improve your enunciation. Or, perhaps you want to speed up or slow down your speaking pace. You might want to be more assertive in stating a request for help. Perhaps you want to eliminate your nervous laugh. Work on your interpersonal style, and set improvement goals in relation to the job search projects you'll accomplish this week.

Little Victories

When we analyze our lives, we focus on big events, major accomplishments, or failures. Everyday life consists of hundreds of small goals, most of which are habitual. We do them without thinking. You'll be setting more challenging goals each day. When you succeed, congratulate yourself. Little victories are the essence of life. These are the things we talk about at the end of the day. They add pleasure to an otherwise routine day.

You have many of reasons to celebrate. You have the courage to move your career in a new direction. You face uncertainties, and you have a great deal to learn. Step by step, you're making progress. Look back to where you started and recognize that you've already completed some of the most difficult parts of the journey. Silence the voice that says, "Yes, but there's so much more to do." Of course there is, but for now, concentrate on planning next week's goals. Recognize you're well on your way.

You can celebrate by yourself, but it's more satisfying to celebrate with friends and family. Tell close friends about the greatest challenges you've set for yourself this week. When you complete these goals, share your happiness. Praise from others will reinforce your efforts and motivate you to set even higher goals for the next week.

If you've never kept a journal, this could be another arena for personal development. Take a few minutes during the day to record your thoughts, feelings, and the lessons you're learning from the job search process. Writing will help bring more ideas to the surface. Take a few minutes to review your notes and acknowledge your progress.

If...Then...

Life is based on a continuing series of *if-then*—cause and effect—events. *If* you study, *then* you'll get a better grade. *If* you rewrite your paper, *then* it's more likely to be published. And, *if* you don't start building your business network, *then* it will take longer to get a job.

You can use if-then contingencies as another source of motivation. What do you enjoy doing at the end of the day? Playing video games? Calling a friend? Walking the dog? Create an incentive. "If I call five people today, then I can play Grand Theft Auto (call Jeneen, or walk Shorty)." When you complete a job search goal, reward yourself.

The problem with setting if-then contingencies is: Who holds you accountable? Accountability adds three words and transforms the contingency into "if, *and only if*, then . . ." You only get the reward if you achieve your goal completely. It's not enough to have tried to do it, or to have completed part of it. No. If, and only if, you complete the *entire* goal can you walk Shorty. Are you able to hold yourself accountable, or do you need someone's help? Most of us need an enforcer. We can always find reasons why we deserve the reward regardless of whether we've fully completed the goal.

Setbacks

There are always obstacles along the way. When you face a major setback, you feel frustration, anger, disappointment, and a sense of helplessness. When setbacks happen in quick succession, you may feel so discouraged you'll want to quit. What do you do when you hit that wall?

You can briefly express your negative feelings, but then you have to go right back to it. As the cloying song lyric says, "Pick yourself up, dust yourself off, and start all over again." When sports commentators make pronouncements about what it will take for a team to win the championship, they rely on the well worn cliché, "They'll have to take their game up a notch to make it to the top." Hackneyed as it sounds, it's true. You can't indulge in endless anger and disappointment. Eventually, you'll have to take action. Why not start now, perhaps in smaller bites?

You have the energy and creativity to overcome any barrier that blocks you from getting a business job. Put your internal resources to work as quickly as possible. You won't be able to draw on this extra energy forever, but you can call upon it for a few days or hours. When you tackle the obstacle again, you'll experience some success. This small victory will enable you to cleanse negative feelings and go after the next challenge.

There may be times when you have to fake it. You just don't feel like working on your goals. Start anyway. Although it may feel laborious, if you keep working, you'll soon make progress. This success will motivate you to keep going, and as the small successes accumulate, you'll feel a sense of accomplishment.

Distractions

When you don't feel like working, the smallest things will nag you and demand immediate attention. The plants look dry; new emails should be checked; the laundry's piling up; Shorty wants to play Frisbee. These small distractions can disrupt your commitment to complete today's list of goals. You have to put these temptations out of sight and out of mind.

Make a list of the sirens that sing out for your attention. Research shows that the most effective way to delay gratification is to shift your attention away from the temptation. Block any enticements from your field of awareness. Putting a temptation out of your sight will help put it out of your mind. You may need to move the plants out of your field of vision. If incoming emails are beeping, or you keep tripping over the pile of laundry, turn off the computer and put the dirty laundry in the hamper.

Get rid of some temptations and use others as carrots in a contingency. "If I talk to three people in my network, then I can play with Shorty." By delaying this pleasure, it becomes a reward.

Self Renewal

This ongoing litany—set goals, work, set more goals, etc.—can be exhausting. If you're searching for a job while still taking grad classes, or conducting research, your workload can become overwhelming. The recommendations in this chapter are meant to encourage rather than admonish you to work, work, work.

You must renew your energy and spirit. No matter how many demands you face each week, you must find an hour or two to have fun and relax. It may be going to a film, reading a novel, watching television, attending a religious service, taking a walk, or enjoying a nice meal. Your energy needs to be replenished. After all you've done this week, schedule a little time for yourself. Not only will you feel better immediately, you'll recharge, refocus, and be more effective when you get back to work.

Savoring the Journey

The attainment of your goal can loom on the horizon and take over your life. Don't let it. Take a few moments every day to reflect on your journey.

This is your life and you are committed to taking control. Savor that declaration. You're accomplishing things you couldn't even imagine last week. You're dong things you couldn't do just a week ago. That's cause for celebration. Record these observations in your journal. They'll be an ongoing source of inspiration and learning.

Monumental as this journey feels to you, other people are facing challenges that are as large as, or greater than yours. These kinds of challenges are part of what it means to be a human being. Take time to recognize your own humanity and the human condition we all share.

24

The End Game

"I'm sorry to tell you, but we selected the other candidate. It was a difficult decision. You have many outstanding qualities and I'm sure you'll be able to get a job. . ." You'll shut out everything once you register the implication of "sorry." If you really wanted this job, and you felt you aced the interview, it's especially devastating. There's very little anyone can say to take away the pain.

While people's words may not provide much comfort, there are other ways you can move forward after your initial disappointment. Disconcerting as the news may be, you can take something positive from the otherwise negative phone call. As soon as the caller is identified, prepare yourself for anything. This can help you remain in control. Try to retain your composure, so you can ask some vital questions. The hiring manager doesn't take any pleasure delivering bad news. Most individuals will answer your calm inquiries.

Begin with a simple, if not completely true, statement. "I regret that I won't have the opportunity to work with you at this time, but I respect your decision. I'd like to learn from this experience. Can I ask a few questions?"

Express your positive feelings for the company and ask if you might learn about any future jobs. See if you can be one of the first to hear about new openings. Next, you can ask which of your characteristics made you especially attractive as a candidate. While this information may be comforting, you'll learn more from your next inquires.

Don't try to convince the hiring manager she made a mistake. This job is gone. Move on. Ask how you might improve your resume and interviewing skills.

Begin by explaining that you're personally committed to the process of *continuous improvement.*

This *debriefing interview,* like the informational interview, is designed solely to gain information, not to get a job. Take notes. You're getting feedback from someone who likes you—they almost hired you. Not only does the hiring manager want to help you, she understands the business hiring process.

Thank her for the suggestions and explain why they're so helpful. If you feel comfortable with the interviewer, ask if you might contact her again. She might have some helpful advice when you interview with another company. In addition to receiving a few tips, the hiring manager is a very valuable addition to your network.

The Worst That Could Happen

Congratulations. You've faced the worst fate, "Sorry, but no." And, you've survived. By conducting a debriefing interview with the hiring manager, you've made the best of a bad situation. You've taken control, and you've gained valuable insights. You can use the information to diagnose your errors and become an even better candidate for your next interview.

Root Cause Analysis

Businesses use a process of continuous improvement to reduce costs and improve quality. Perfecting performance depends on finding and correcting the source of the problems. You can use the information from the debriefing interview to isolate aspects of your performance that need to be improved. Often there are multiple contributory causes. Once they're identified, it's possible to take corrective action.

Insufficient Experience

You already knew your lack of experience could be an impediment. The good news is, your other attributes were sufficiently strong that the company wanted to take a serious look at you.

How can you get more experience? You need to specify whether your overall lack of business experience, or a lack of experience in the company's industry, contributed to the hiring manager's decision. Almost any part-time or fulltime job will help eradicate a lack of familiarity with business.

Insufficient Industry Knowledge

You're caught in a Catch 22 if your problem is a lack of industry experience. You can't get a job until you have experience, and since you don't have experience, you can't get a job. The only option is an internship, or volunteering to work for free at a company in the industry.

Even as you continue to apply for jobs in the industry, become an expert by doing more and more research. Read trade publications and media analyses of the industry and its future. Arrange informational interviews, so you become more familiar with the mindset of insiders. In the next go-around, you may be even more knowledgeable than the interviewer.

You might also take courses in your prospective career area. Informational interviews will add to your knowledge of issues and jargon. The more knowledge the better, but it's still not the same as working in the field.

Lack of Fit with the Company Culture

This is seldom the sole reason you might be passed over. Perhaps you may think of yourself as hard driving, risk oriented, and having strong people skills, but somehow it didn't come across. It's a judgment call, and unfortunately we know who always wins this debate.

Take a fresh look at yourself and the characteristics (e.g., hard driving) the interviewer termed "less than a perfect fit." Ask people in your network for their opinion. Although people may agree that you're hard driving, it's not being adequately conveyed.

If your network's judgment is that you aren't exceptionally hard driving, you'll have to make some adjustments. It may be difficult to believe the interviewer did you a favor, but perhaps you would not have fit after all. Painful as it may have been to hear, you now have a better sense of who you are and where you should look for a job.

Lack of a Personal Connection with the Interviewer

No employer will be this blunt, but perhaps you didn't connect on a personal level. Sometimes there isn't a spark, and there's little you can do about it. The more common reason interviewers don't connect, however, is that they don't feel the candidate has a genuine commitment to the job. You have to convince them you want *this* job. Put your passion into words and action.

It's tempting to invent extraneous reasons for a lack of connection. The interviewer went to a rival college, doesn't like women (men), was intimidated by your graduate education, etc. Maybe, but it's unlikely. Interviewers are very professional, and they almost always look past any superficiality. If you're still convinced the spark just wasn't there, pay more attention to subtle signals your next interviewer sends about his interests. Use these cues to establish a bond at the beginning of the interview.

Poor Interview Performance

You have to get down to ground level if this is the culprit. Were you nervous or too relaxed, inarticulate or too polished, overly confident or lacking in confidence? Did you have an attitude of superiority, or did you project a sense of unworthiness? Arrange several more mock interviews, and ask people to be 100% honest in their evaluations. You'll want to eradicate any negative behaviors and replace them with positive actions. The more you practice, the more your anxiety level will drop.

Did you think the content of your answers was in any way inadequate? Did you have too much or too little to say? Were you overly detailed or too general? Did you stumble over your answers, or contradict yourself? Work on refining your answers to common interview questions. Rewrite and polish your answers. Develop more concrete and compelling behavioral examples. Practice new ways to illustrate how your strengths will help a company move forward.

The next time you have an interview, you may need to more thoroughly research the company. Learn everything you can about the company and the industry. Write concise summaries of what you've learned. Frame your opinions about the future of the company and the industry in optimistic terms. Also, carefully develop a set of questions for the interviewer. Pretend you're looking through binoculars. You want to bring the job and the industry into precise focus.

Budgeting Your Time

Time can slip away when you're not employed. Research has documented the daily activities of adults who are employed and those who are looking for work. Data from the 2008 American Time Use Survey highlights these differences. It's not surprising employed people work on average an additional 6 hours each day. The unemployed spend an extra 2 hours per day on home/personal chores, and another two hours socializing. One additional hour per day is consumed with television, education and sleeping.

Are you prone to allowing nonproductive activities to consume your day? It takes discipline to become efficient while working from home. Some people need to get dressed as though they were going off to work, while others are productive in pajamas. Morning people and night people find ways to adapt their work schedules to their body rhythms. The one thing they have in common—they schedule specific hours to work. Finding a job is a job. You'll have to establish a routine and habits that enable you to be productive.

Luck, Fate, Timing, Kismet and Karma

Up until now, this book has presented a very rational model of the job search process. There are tools and resources you must develop, and then use, to systematically locate a job. This is the accepted approach—it will produce a job.

While you're busy working on this process, other elements will invariably come into play. Call it fate or luck, these elements are outside your control and yet they can determine your success. Dressed in your grubby T-shirt and raggedy jeans, you go to the market late one night for some ice cream. To your amazement, you meet an old friend from high school. After you get reacquainted and catch up on family and friends, you casually mention you're looking for a job. She gives you a look of amazement and says, "You won't believe this, but my company is about to hire an assistant project manager. You'd be perfect!"

This woman isn't in your network, she hasn't seen your resume, you certainly aren't dressed for success—but lo and behold, the phone rings the next day and suddenly you've got an interview.

This kind of story is told over and over because it actually happens. And, it might happen to you. Another possible scenario goes like this: You take a part-time job on the weekend. It's a stockroom job and doesn't require much thought or energy. The money is good, and you're paid in cash. As the weeks go by, you develop a casual friendship with one of your co-workers. One day he mentions that his dad rides in a car pool. His dad is friendly with a really nice guy who's putting together a new company. Your friend gives you his father's phone number and two weeks later, you're working full time.

Factors outside one's control often play an important role in determining the path to a career. It's fair to say that for about 50% of job seekers, fate is the primary variable. Does this mean you should give up your systematic search? Absolutely not. All the work you're doing will make it possible to take advantage of any fortuitous opportunity. When fate walks in the door, you'll be ready.

You have a resume, business card, elevator pitch, list of questions, and correct business attire. You've done your research. You know the industry and you know your strengths. You can speak the language of business and you have a career strategy. If you have the good fortune to experience such a fateful encounter, you can hand out your business card, email a resume, and begin researching the company.

Now imagine this scenario: You aren't prepared. You've been putting off writing a resume, you've lost touch with your S&A group, and the information on your business card is completely outdated. One night, you go to the market for ice cream and you meet the same high school acquaintance. And presto— nothing happens. You've missed an opportunity, and you'll probably miss the next one, too.

Success is the result of luck + hard work. The reality is that one way or another, you *will* get a job. You might find it through an internet website, an ad in the newspaper, the career center at your university, *or* through a chance meeting with an old friend.

Keep working on your job skills, gain as much information as possible and be prepared—for the ad that catches your eye, or for the golden opportunity that changes your life. Either way, you *will* successfully move from *Academics* to *Business*. Bravo!

Index